Embroidering Happiness

PATTERNS AND PROJECTS FOR LIFE'S EVERYDAY TREASURES

Yula

Introduction

In this book, I wanted to capture the things I love from everyday life in embroidery. Surrounded by such treasures, I embroider those same things. I hope you will enjoy the designs in this book as much as I do.

May these embroidery patterns delight you.
May they bring your attention to the pleasure found in everyday things.
May you find the happiness that I have found in embroidery.

Contents

Plants

Plants and flowers are the most common motifs in embroidery. I love stitching together bouquets of little flowers—they are so delightful.

Make the embroidered fabric into a ribbon and tie it into a headband. You can also make just the ribbon and fasten it onto a store-bought headband.

1-a Headband (Blossoms)

Project instructions and pattern | pp. 50, 51

Tie up a bundle of forget-me-nots with a ribbon. I enclosed these in an oval embroidery frame.

2 Embroidery Frame

Pattern | p. 53

This tote bag features a wreath of forget-me-nots. The handles are slightly longer, making it easy to carry bundles.

3 Tote Bag (Forget-Me-Nots)

Project instructions and pattern | pp. 54, 56

This pattern includes a variety of budding leaves. Revel in all the different shades of green!

4-a Green Leaves

Pattern | p. 60

This drawstring pouch is not at all difficult to assemble: Simply add a round bottom to two panels of the Green Leaves pattern, and it comes together easily.

4-b Round-Bottomed Drawstring Pouch (Green Leaves)

Project instructions and pattern | pp. 58, 60

You can never have too many of these paperback-sized book covers—and they make ideal gifts. Adjust the size as needed to fit your favorite books.

5 | 6 Book Cover

Project instructions and pattern | pp. 62, 63

There is quite a variety of flowers bundled together in this wreath. I find the combination of white and green so refreshing.

7 Wreath of White Flowers

Pattern | p. 57

8 | 9 Tote Bag and Drawstring Pouch (Florets)

Project instructions and patterns | pp. 54, 55, 56, 88

Adorn this tote with a wreath of these off-white flowers or decorate the pouch with a circle of tiny blooms.

I picked out paired motifs from the samplers and embroidered them on these pouches. Choose your own favorite patterns and arrange them in a way that pleases you.

10-a Pouches (Flowerpots)

Project instructions and pattern | pp. 64, 65

11-a Round-Bottomed Drawstring Pouch (Leaves and Stems)

Project instructions and patterns | pp. 58, 59, 61

12 Baby's Breath

Pattern | p. 66

Since there's no need to change out the color of the thread when working one-color embroidery, you can just relax and stitch away to your heart's content. You can almost hear the rustling of the leaves.

Baby's breath in a bouquet or two or three, or in a wreath, or hanging to be dried—it looks just like a flower shop.

13 A Path Through the Forest

Pattern | p. 67

In the forest, there are so many plants and trees
that make for excellent embroidery designs.
Breathe in deeply as you wander along the path.

Daily Life

These are cherished items from our daily lives.
The more familiar, the dearer these things are to us.

14 Kitchen

Pattern | p. 68

A frying pan, a Dutch oven, a tea kettle, and a pitcher—when they're arranged like this, don't they look like they belong in a still-life painting?

15 **Breakfast**

Pattern | p. 69

Start the morning off simply—take care to choose the finest ingredients, and you'll be all set for the day.

Fresh vegetables are nature's gift of the seasons. I sketched these as I watched them grow into healthy plants.

16-a Pot Holder (Vegetables)

Project instructions and pattern | pp. 70, 71

17-a Socks

Pattern | p. 73

You can be as adventurous as you like with different patterns and colors for these socks. Socks are fun because they offer a hint of your style through just a peek of your feet!

18 Stationery

Pattern | p. 74

The functional design of stationery is what makes it so cool. It's no wonder that so many of these items have long inspired our obsessions.

Bon voyage! Safe travels! And then, *Welcome home!* This design will make you feel glad to venture out today.

19-a Welcome

Pattern | p. 76

20-a Knitted Hats

Pattern | p. 78

A knitted woolen hat is the perfect companion for cold weather. Which pattern will you knit for the coming season?

These mittens keep your hands warm, of course, but they're also so cute. I love to see them lined up like this. This design is perfect for a cup holder.

21-a | 21-b Mittens, Cup Holder

Project instructions and patterns | pp. 80, 81, 82

Favorite Things

Fresh fruits, bread right out of the oven, and sweet treats—
these delicious things are as dear to me as embroidery.

22 Cherries

Pattern | p. 75

I scattered these sweet, tart cherries so that it looks like they're sprinkled all over the pattern.

23 Bread

Pattern | p. 83

When it's time to take a break, a sweet treat is a must. Which one will you enjoy today?

24-a Magnets (Sweet Treats)

Project instructions and pattern | p. 84

I started to assemble my favorite kinds of bread for this design, and soon there were so many that I had to make them into a wreath.

Add a selection from a pattern of your choice to a wide grosgrain ribbon. There's no need to finish the ends, so this is an easy project.

25-a Ribbon (Mushrooms)

Pattern | p. 86

Dare to use unexpected colors for these mushroom caps. Somehow such unusual hues don't seem out of place at all.

25-b Drawstring Pouch (Mushrooms)

Project instructions and pattern | pp. 87, 88, 89

26 Drawstring Pouch (Watermelon)

Project instructions and pattern | pp. 88, 89, 90

27 Drawstring Pouch (Pears)

Project instructions and pattern | pp. 88, 89, 90

When it comes to watermelon, a sliced wedge is the quintessential image that comes to mind. This pattern has these motifs scattered across the fabric. The drawstring pouch project has an oblong shape and a gusset so a bento box or container can fit inside, making it usable as a lunch bag.

The delicate curves of the pears are beautiful, and their cross sections look like still-life paintings. I made this pouch a full size larger than the watermelon version.

Samplers

I gathered together an assortment of motifs for each of these themes. You can work these as is, change up the colors, or even pull out one motif as an accent for a project.

28

Atelier

Pattern | p. 91

29

Gardening

Pattern | p. 92

30

Cookies

Pattern | p. 93

31

Bakery

Pattern | p. 94

32

Teatime

Pattern | p. 95

10-b

Flowerpots

Pattern | p. 65

1-b Blossoms

Pattern | p. 52

16-b

Vegetables

Pattern | p. 72

24-b

Sweet Treats

Pattern | p. 85

17-b

Socks

Pattern | p. 73

21-c

Mittens

Pattern | p. 82

19-b

Welcome

Pattern | p. 77

20-b

Knitted Hats

Pattern | p. 79

Embroidery Basics & Fundamentals

MATERIALS AND TOOLS

A Fabric: There are many fabrics that can be used for needlework—basically any fabric that is pliable—but most of the embroidery patterns in this book call for plain-weave linen.

B Fusible Interfacing: Add fusible interfacing to the reverse side of your ground fabric as a lining. For dark fabric colors, use black fusible interfacing.

C Fusible Quilt Batting: For embroidered projects that will be displayed on a panel, I add a layer of fusible quilt batting. This is also used for the pot holders.

D Embroidery Floss: For most of the projects in this book, I used DMC No. 25 embroidery floss.

E Embroidery Hoops: This tool is used to stretch fabric tightly. I like to wrap the outer hoop with fabric so that the metal doesn't leave a mark on the fabric.

F Needles: I use French embroidery needles, Nos. 3–7, depending on the number of strands of embroidery floss.

G Basting Pins: Use these for temporarily holding parts of your projects in place.

H Needle Threader: This tool makes it easier to put the thread into the eye of even the finest of needles.

I Tracing Table/Light Box: When tracing patterns onto white fabric, place the pattern on this to make it transparent.

J Tracing Paper and Cellophane: Layer these over patterns when tracing them.

K Embroidery Transfer Paper: I use this paper to transfer patterns onto fabric. The kind branded specifically for embroidery is best.

L Tracer: This tool is used to trace the pattern when transferring onto fabric. You can also use a ballpoint pen that has run out of ink.

M Water-Soluble Chacopen: Use this for tracing finer details in patterns. This Chacopen's ink can be erased or washed out.

N Triangle Tailor's Chalk: A powdery chalk variation is useful when drawing long, straight lines.

O Scissors: The large scissors are used for fabric and the small scissors are used for cutting out patterns and such. I use *nigiri hasami* snip scissors for cutting embroidery floss and thread.

P Basting Clips: These are great to use for bigger areas than can be held by basting pins.

Q Bodkin: Use this to thread the drawstrings through casings on a pouch.

R Eyeleteer: I like to use this for making neat corners on bags and pouches.

S Stay Tape: Use this (0.9-cm diameter) on the opening of a pouch to keep it from losing shape.

T Cutting Mat: Place this underneath your work when tracing patterns to avoid damaging the surface of your desk or table.

U Basting Thread: This is helpful to use when tracing patterns or for marking the finished edge of patterns with complicated shapes.

Another Useful Item

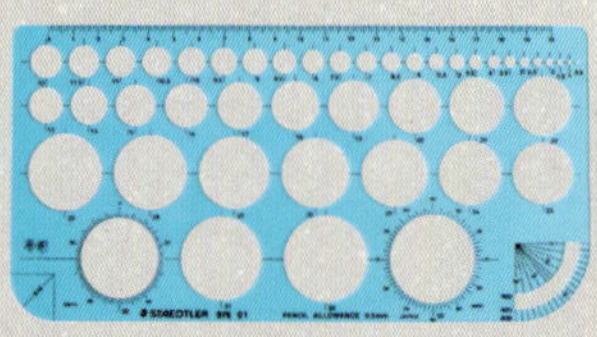

Circle Stencil Template: This tool helps you draw precise circles of many sizes.

How to Handle No. 25 Embroidery Thread

No. 25 embroidery thread comes with six strands intertwined. You'll need to separate these fine strands based on the number of strands indicated in the pattern.

1. Pull a standard length of 50–60 cm from the skein, and cut the thread.
2. One at a time, untangle and separate the six strands. They will become twisted again while you are stitching, so continue to untangle them every so often.
3. Arrange the number of strands you need, parallel, with the ends aligned together neatly. Fold the strands over your embroidery needle and then thread them through the eye.

HOW TO TRACE PATTERNS

For anything other than white fabric, use embroidery transfer paper. For white fabric, use tracing paper.

1. Before tracing the pattern, add fusible interfacing to the reverse side of your ground fabric. Secure the edges so that it won't peel apart.
2. Place tracing paper over the pattern and use a pencil or whatever tool you prefer. (For white fabric, place the pattern on the tracing table, then layer the fabric over it and trace the pattern directly onto the fabric.)
3. Layer in this order: Place embroidery transfer paper over the fabric followed by the tracing paper, the pattern, and the cellophane. Then transfer the pattern with your tracing tool.

Tips for Tracing Patterns

A Since you'll be embroidering over the pattern and it won't be visible over your work, I recommend tracing over the finer details of the pattern with a Chacopen.

B For evenly spaced petals on flowers, I use a circle as a guideline. To avoid making distorted circles, I simply mark their positions with a dot and then later use a stencil template to draw them with a Chacopen. You can also just trace the lines of the petals and draw in a circle later using a Chacopen.

C In the patterns, French knots are shown as circles to make it easy to imagine the finished stitch, but you can just mark the center with a dot.

D Patterns with finely detailed areas include guidelines. To ensure a neat shape, it can be helpful to trace these as well, but since they tend to disappear while stitching, I like to mark them with basting thread. Just be careful not to work outside the lines, and your finished project will be neat and clean.

A

B

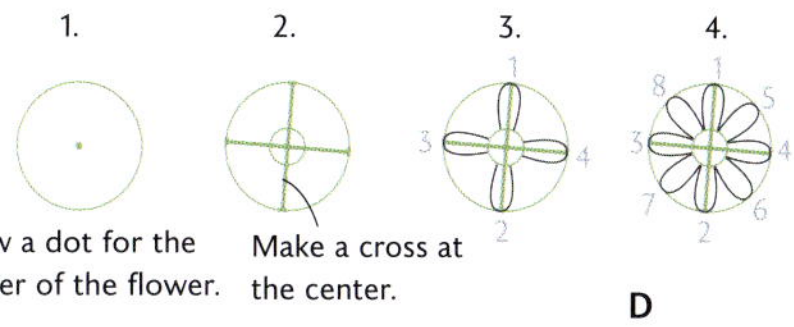

C

D

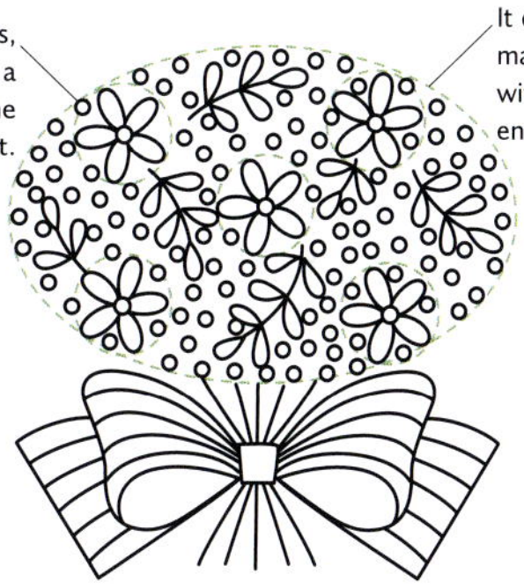

SEQUENCE OF STITCHING

E Ideally, the best sequence for stitches is to start by creating outlines so the tracings will not be erased or disappear. I start by working the lines in any motifs, such as stems for leaves. Once you have first worked the outlines, you can go back and fill in areas with chain or satin stitches, then finish the finer details. I always work French knot stitches last.

E

STARTING AND ENDING YOUR EMBROIDERY

F & G Generally, I don't make knots in my embroidery. When starting, I leave about 10 cm of thread from the starting point, then I work my stitches. Once I've finished, I clean up by weaving in the ends. The same goes for ending my embroidery. If you're worried about it, feel free to make knots.

- Anchoring the thread vertically: Turn your work over, weave the thread through your stitches two or three times, then trim the end.
- Anchoring the thread horizontally: On the reverse side, pass the thread under your stitches one or two times, then trim the end.

F

G

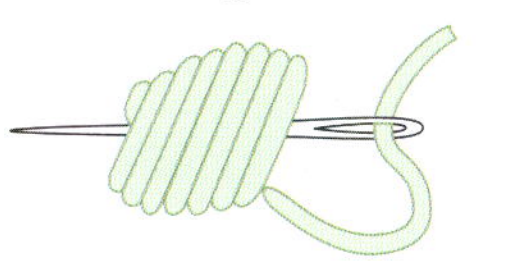

Stitching Tips

HOW TO STITCH FLOWER PETALS WITH SATIN STITCHES

1 Begin by working satin stitches outward from the center of the pattern.

2 As the petals widen, start by stitching from the center of the petal, then add stitches on each side.

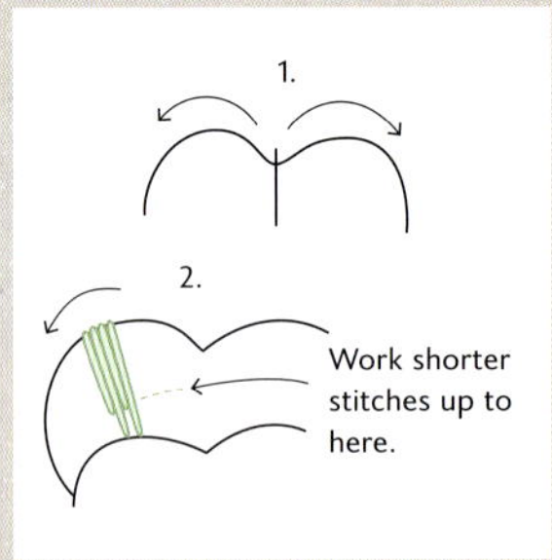

1. Work one stitch in the center.
2. Since the size of the outer petals is larger, adjust the length of your stitches.

3 Since the edges are curved, work your outline stitches finely to create a neat border.

HOW TO STITCH FLOWER PETALS WITH CHAIN STITCHES

1 Work outline stitches around the border.
* In curved areas, work your stitches finely to create a neat line.

2 Work one row of chain stitches just along the inside of the outline stitches.

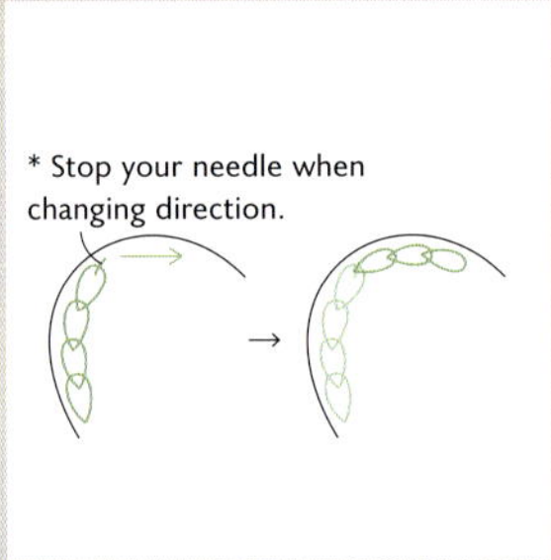

When you reach the point on the curve where the angle turns, stop your needle, then continue stitching by bringing it up inside the next chain stitch.

3 Fill in the rest of the area with chain stitches.

HOW TO STITCH MINIATURE ROSES

1 Work three parallel straight stitches in the center.

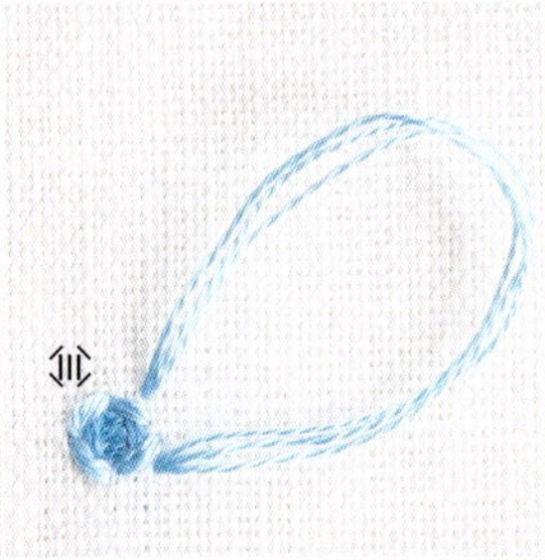

2 Add straight stitches at each corner.

3 Once the shape starts to round, add outline stitches.

HOW TO FILL IN LEAVES WITH CHAIN STITCHES

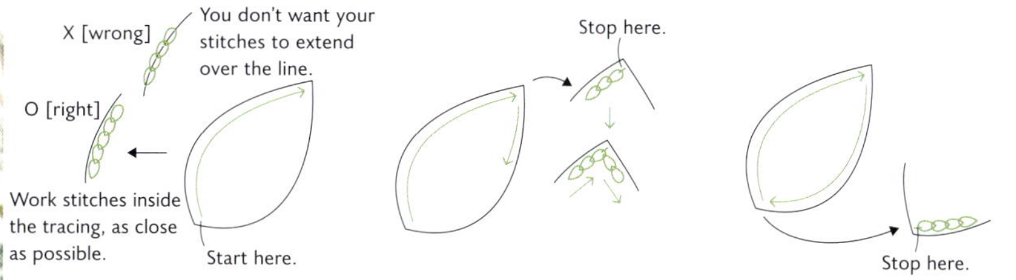

1 Work stitches inside the tracing, as close as possible, rather than extending over the marking.

2 When you reach an angle, stop your needle and change direction.

3 Once you've completed a circuit, stop your needle. Fill in the rest of the area and then work the stem using an outline stitch.

HOW TO WORK BORDERS WITH OUTLINE STITCHES AND THEN FILL IN WITH CHAIN STITCHES

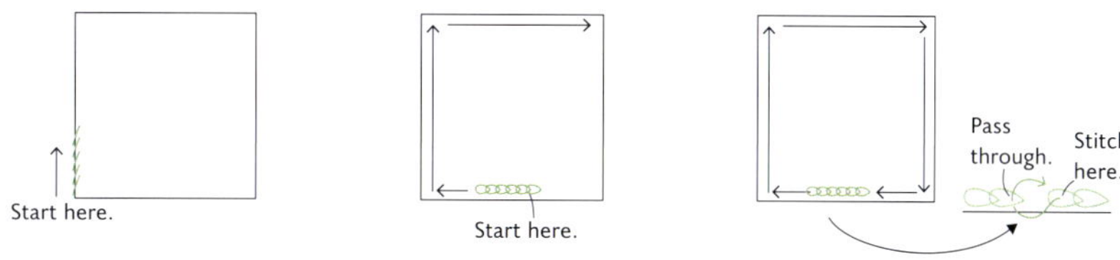

1 Work outline stitches along the tracing.

2 Work chain stitches. When you reach an angle, stop your needle and change direction.

3 Finish by passing your needle through the first stitch, then stop.

HOW TO FILL IN SPIRAL SHAPES WITH CHAIN STITCHES

1 Fill in the circle by working chain stitches from outside to inside.

2 Once the area is filled in, work a spiral line in chain stitch over filled-in stitches.

HOW TO FILL IN TREES WITH CHAIN STITCHES

1 Work the border with outline stitches.

2 Fill in the area inside with chain stitches.

3 Work lines for the branches and trunk in outline stitch over filled-in stitches.

4 Fill in the trunk with chain stitches.

Embroidery Stitches Used in This Book

OUTLINE STITCH

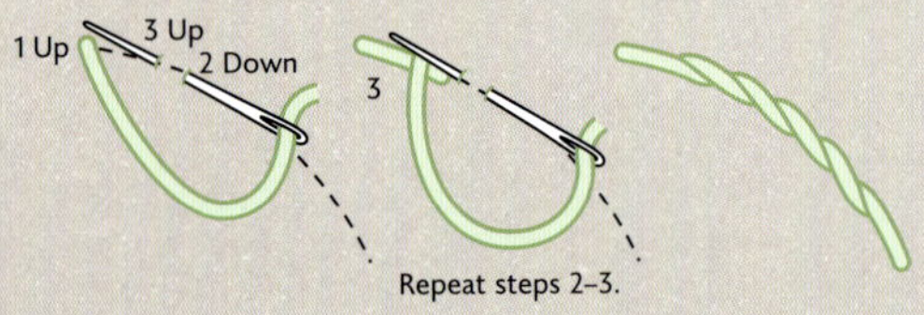

SATIN STITCH

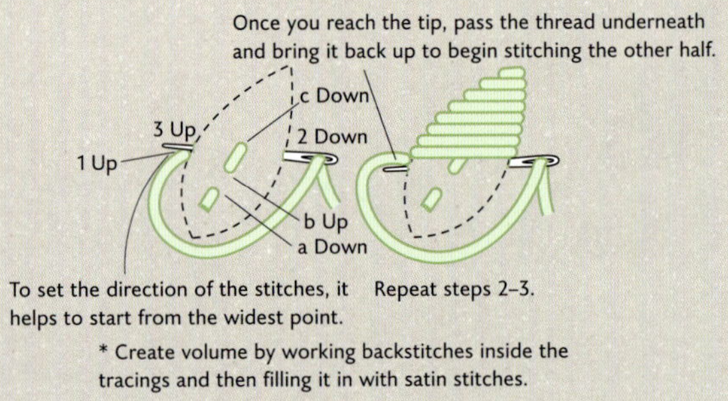

STRAIGHT STITCH

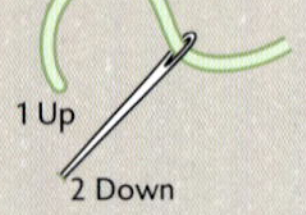

CHAIN STITCH

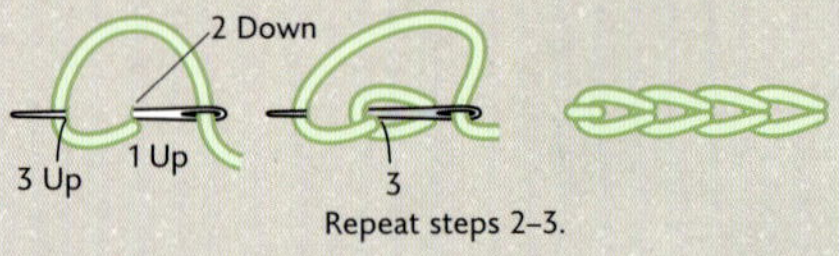

FISHBONE STITCH

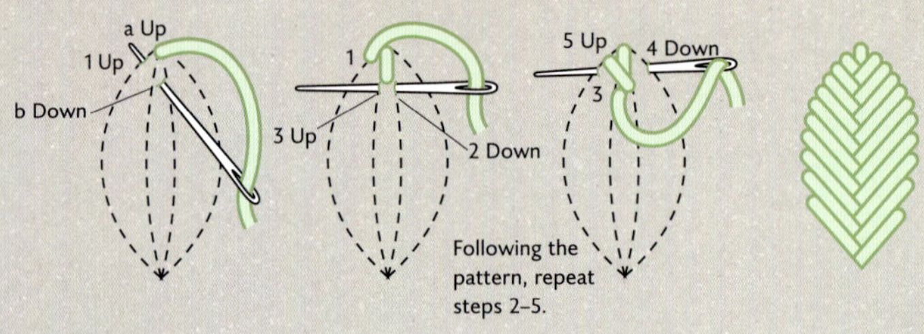

FRENCH KNOT STITCH (DOUBLE WRAP)

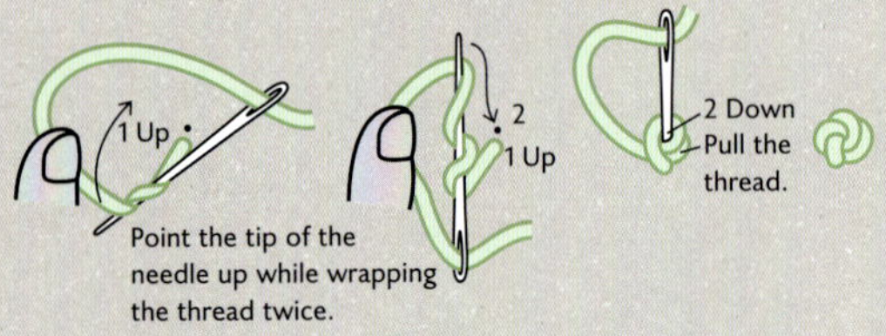

RUNNING STITCH

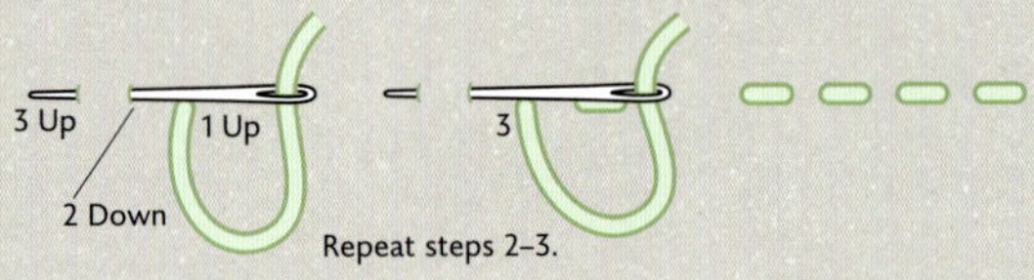

LAZY DAISY STITCH

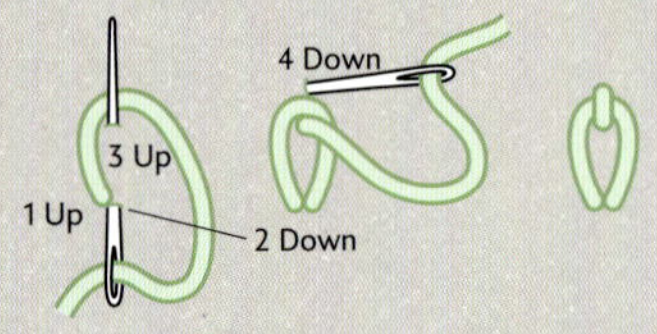

WORK STRAIGHT STITCH OVER LAZY DAISY STITCH.

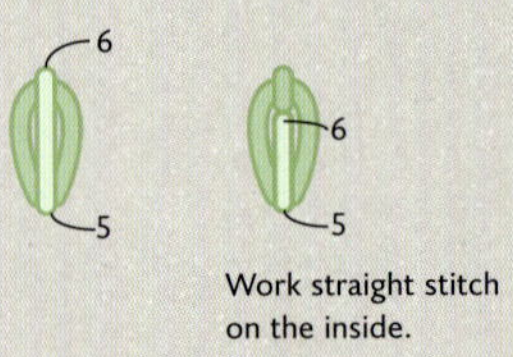

Project Instructions and Patterns

HOW TO READ THE PATTERNS

Each pattern includes a variety of stitches. Generally, stitch instructions are listed as the kind of stitch, the color code for the embroidery floss, and the number of strands.

- All embroidery floss used in this book is DMC No. 25 embroidery floss.
- For projects that you hope to use in your daily life or have around for a long time, it's helpful to add fusible interfacing to the reverse side of your ground fabric as a lining. Since shrinking or puckering can occur with linen after fusing the interfacing and working in the embroidery, it's best to add an extra 5–10 cm of linen to the finished measurements and then, once you've completed the embroidery, trim the excess fabric.
- Once you've completed your embroidery, remove any water-soluble marks by misting lightly with water and dabbing with a cotton swab. Place a cloth over your work and press lightly with a steam iron to finish.
- The numbers shown in the instruction diagrams indicate measurements in centimeters.
- Instruction diagrams and paper patterns do not include seam allowances. Please always add a 1-cm seam allowance all around for your projects.

1-a Headband (Blossoms) | p. 5

Finished measurements: 5 cm wide x approximately 60 cm around

MATERIALS

No. 25 embroidery floss (refer to pattern for color codes)

Fabric: Linen, gray, 60 x 60 cm

Other: Fusible interfacing, 40 x 15 cm; 2-cm-wide elastic, 13 cm

RIBBON

* Add 1-cm seam allowance.

(Cut one piece each for exterior and interior fabric.)

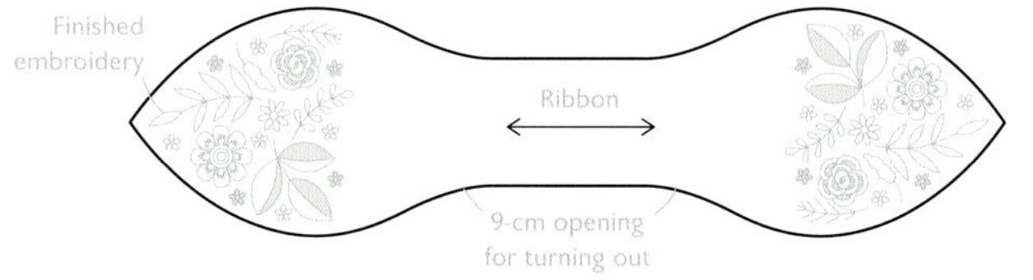

* Fold the exterior fabric in half and align the folded edge precisely with the edge of the paper pattern, then cut the fabric. Attach the fusible interfacing to the reverse side of the finished embroidery.

HEADBAND

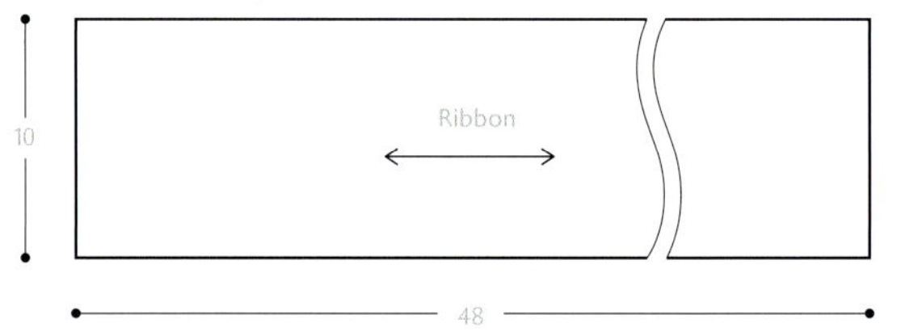

ELASTIC COVERING

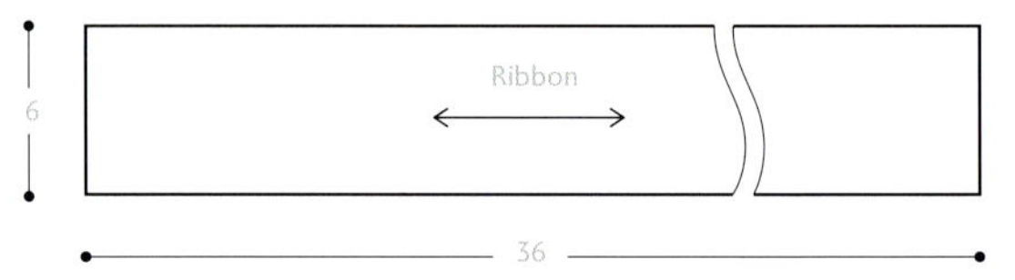

[Ribbon] Assemble the exterior fabric and interior fabric, right sides together, and sew the edges together.

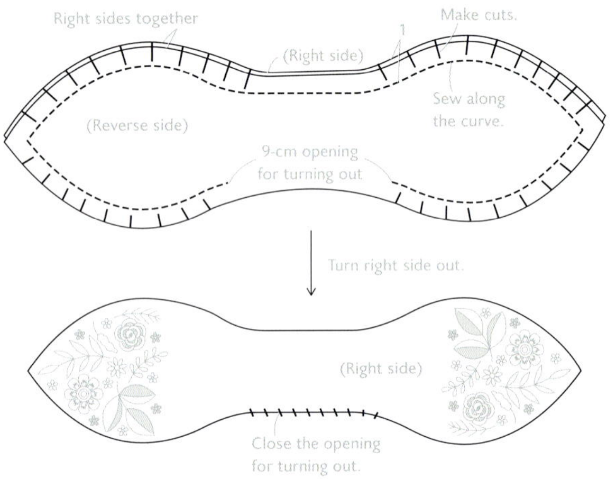

[HEADBAND • ELASTIC COVERING]

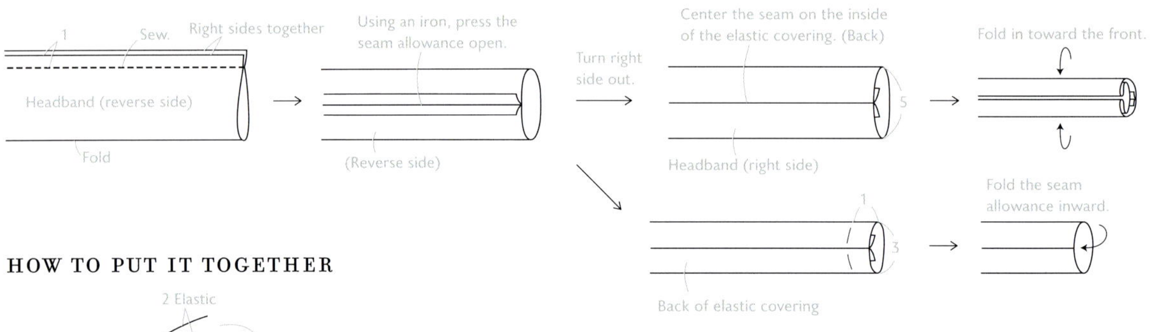

HOW TO PUT IT TOGETHER

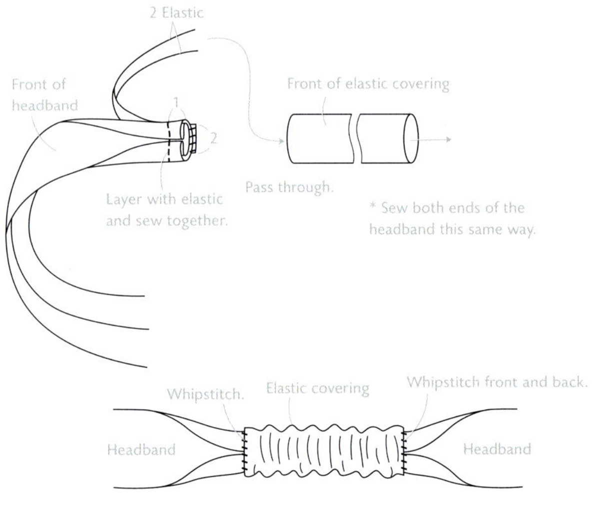

FINISHED PROJECT

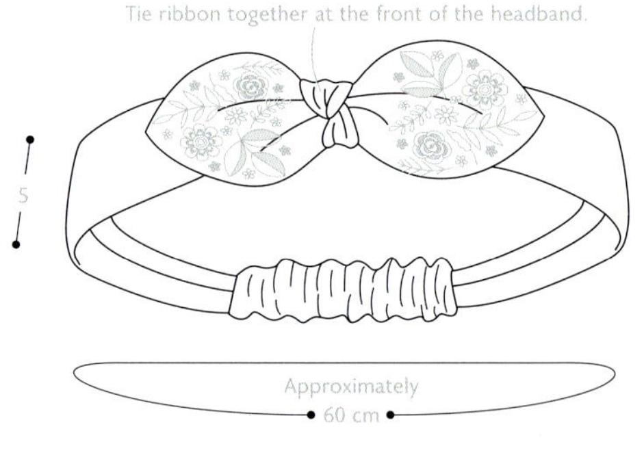

Fold
Paper pattern for ribbon
Lazy daisy + straight 561 (6)
Lazy daisy + straight 326 (4)
French knot 3832 (3)
Outline 3781 (3)
Fill in with chain stitches 367 (2).
Fill in with chain stitches 989 (2).
Outline 10 (3)
Outline 3863 (2)
Lazy daisy + straight 3813 (4)
Work the outline of the shape with outline stitches 335 (2), then work inside the outline with chain stitches 335 (2). Refer to p. 46.
(3)
French knot 3823 (3)
Chain 761 (2)
Fill in with French knot stitches 739 (6).
French knot, from center: 712 (2), 3833 (4), 761 (6)
Outline 3013 (3)
Straight 3832 (2)
Satin 326 (2)
Outline 3862 (3)
Lazy daisy + straight 153 (5)
Center: French knot 3836 (3)
Fill in with chain stitches 472 (2).

1-b Blossoms | p. 40

* Enlarge pattern by 150%.

2 Embroidery Frame | p. 6

Actual size
Once embroidery is finished,
place your work in an oval frame
(DMC MV0034/175 used here).

3 Tote Bag (Forget-Me-Nots) | p. 7

Pattern | p. 56
Finished measurements: 18 x 18 cm

8 Tote Bag (Florets) | p. 12

Pattern | p. 56
Finished measurements: 18 x 18 cm

MATERIALS (TO MAKE ONE TOTE)

No. 25 embroidery floss
(refer to pattern for color codes)

Fabric: Exterior fabric, linen, 40 x 75 cm;
lining fabric, cotton, 20 x 45 cm

Other: Fusible interfacing, 40 x 35 cm

8 Exterior fabric (Cut two pieces.)

* Add 1-cm seam allowance.

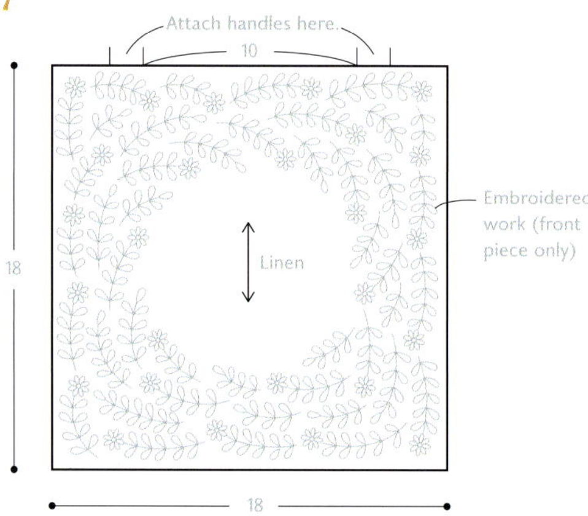

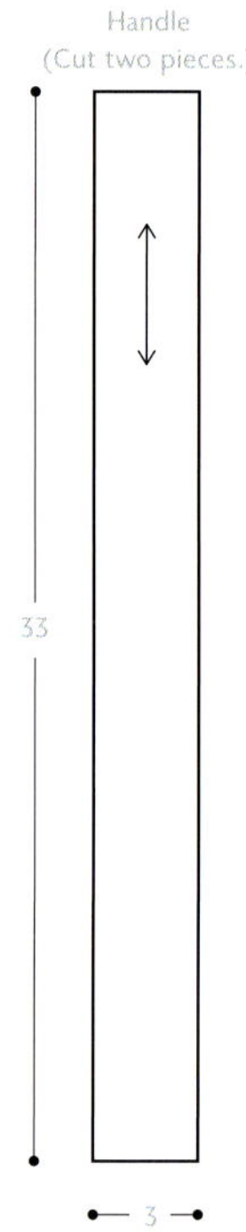

3 Exterior fabric (Cut two pieces.)

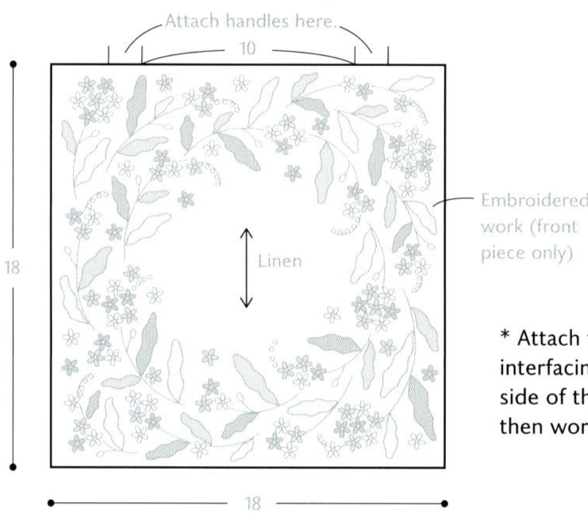

* Attach the fusible interfacing to the reverse side of the exterior fabric, then work embroidery.

Facing (Cut two pieces.)

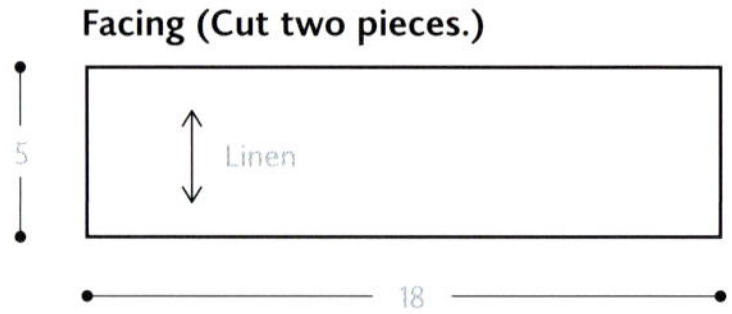

Lining (Cut two pieces.)

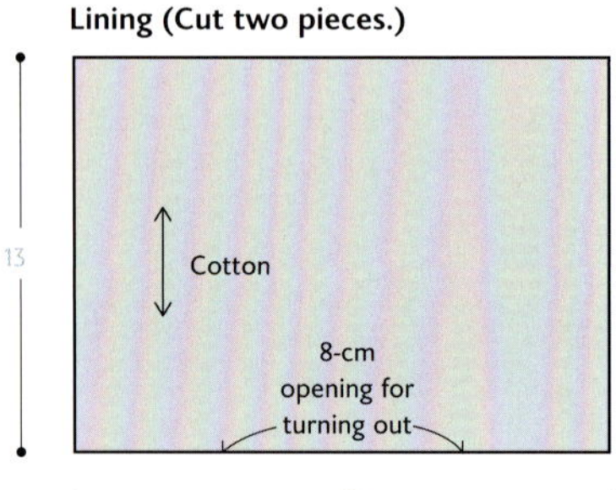

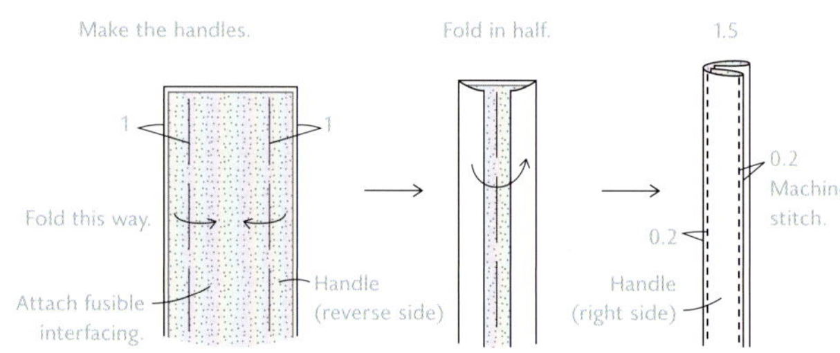

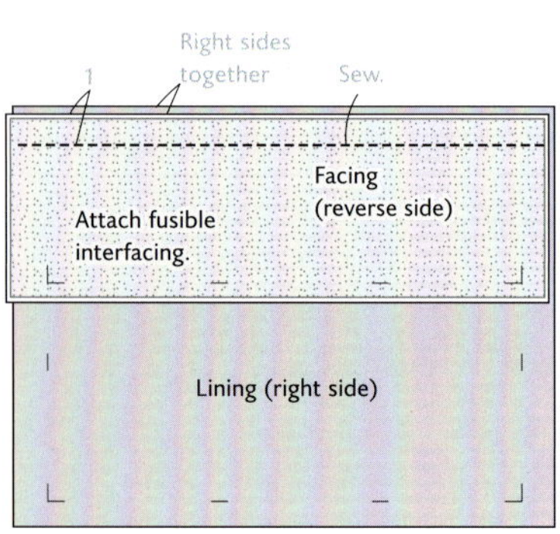

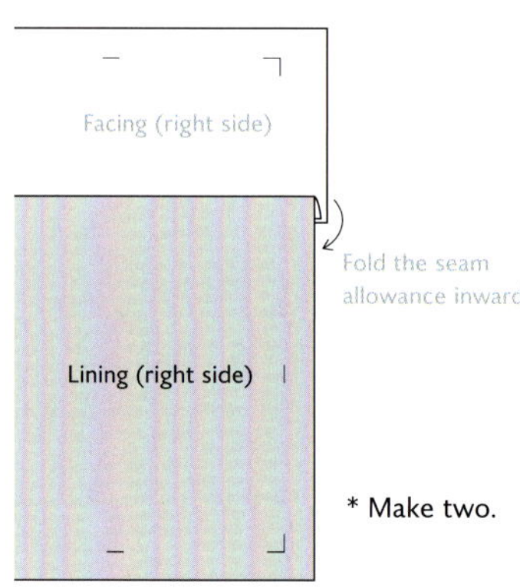

* Make two.

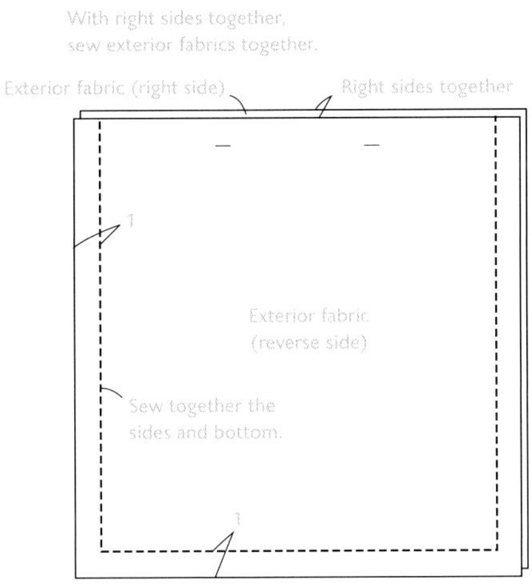

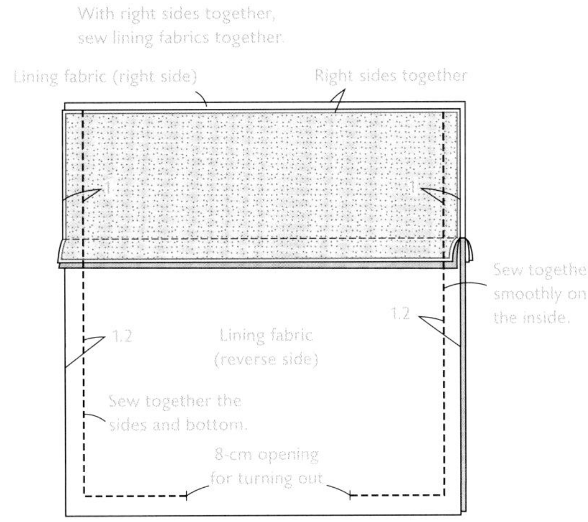

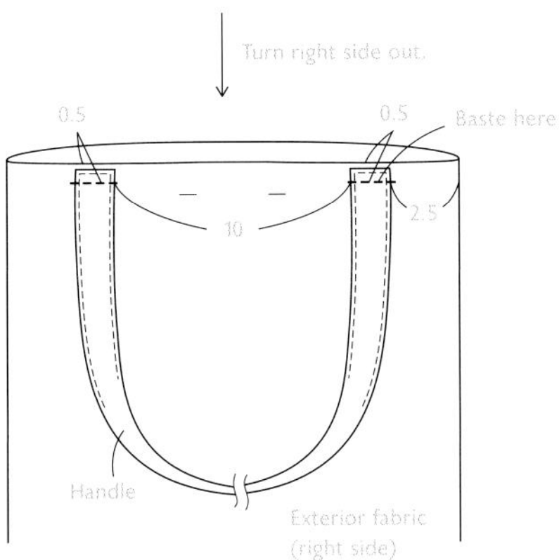

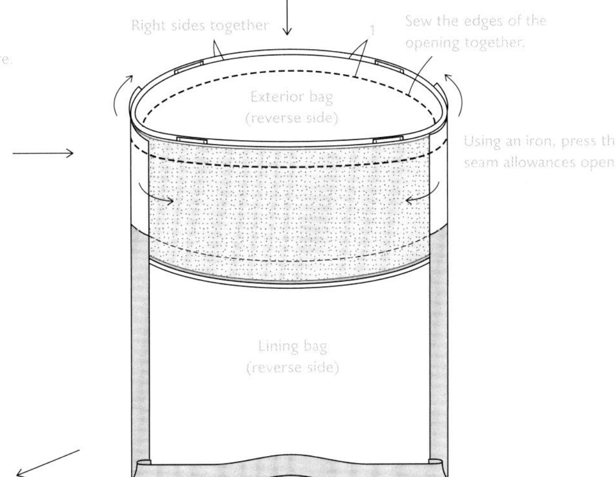

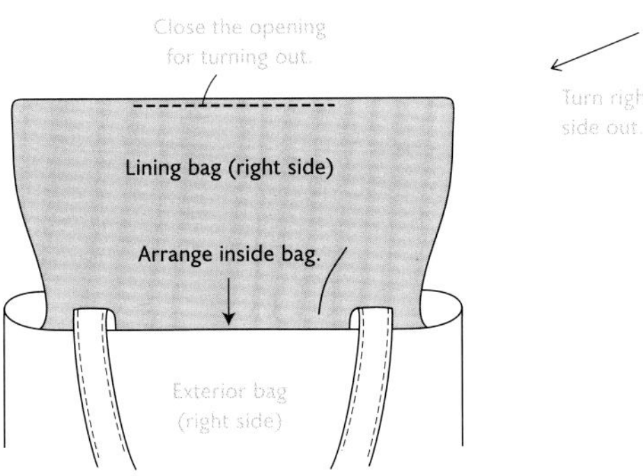

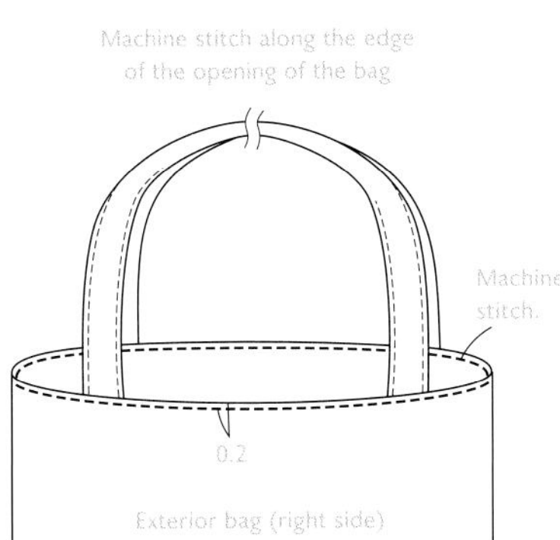

FINISHED PROJECT

3 8 9 Tote Bags and Drawstring Pouch | pp. 7, 12

Project instructions | p. 54 (3 • 8), p. 88 (9)

Enlarge pattern for 3 • 8 by 200%.
Pattern for 9 is actual size.

3

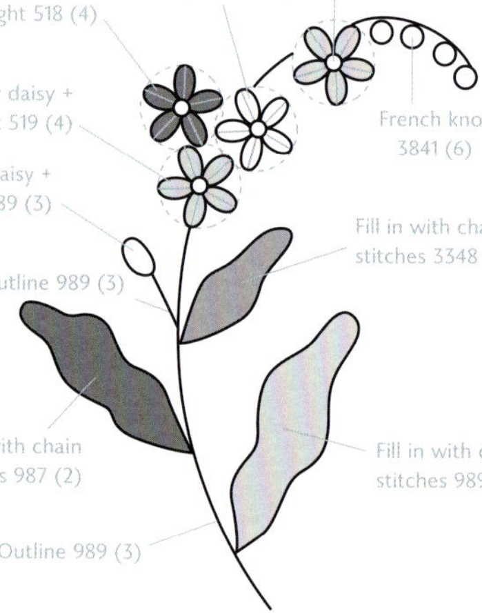

8

9

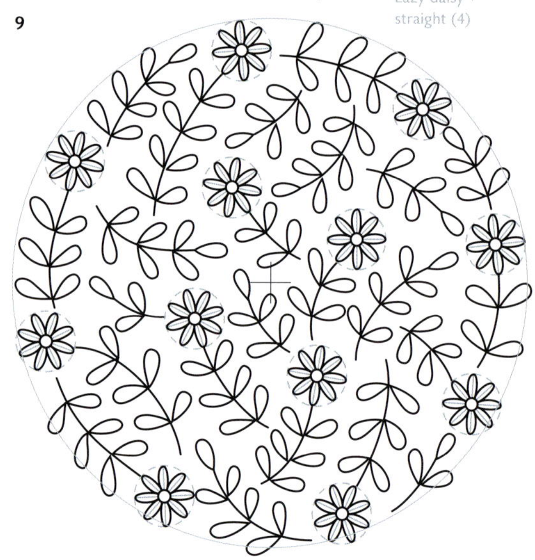

7 Wreath of White Flowers | p. 11

Pattern (actual size)

4-b Round-Bottomed Drawstring Pouch (Green Leaves) | p. 9

Pattern | p. 60
Finished measurements: approximately 19 cm with bottom diameter 10.5 cm

11-a Round-Bottomed Drawstring Pouch (Leaves and Stems) | p. 14

Pattern | p. 61
Finished measurements: approximately 19 cm with bottom diameter 10.5 cm

MATERIALS (TO MAKE ONE POUCH)

No. 25 embroidery floss (refer to pattern for color codes)
Fabric: Exterior fabric, linen, 35 x 65 cm; lining fabric, cotton/linen blend, 20 x 50 cm
Other: Fusible interfacing, 25 x 50 cm; cord, 120 cm

Bottom (Cut one piece each from exterior fabric and lining fabric.)

* Add 1-cm seam allowance.

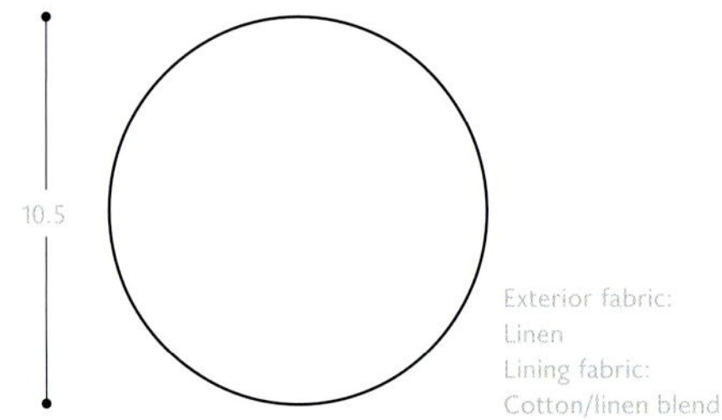

4 Exterior fabric (Cut two pieces.)

Follow same directions for 11.

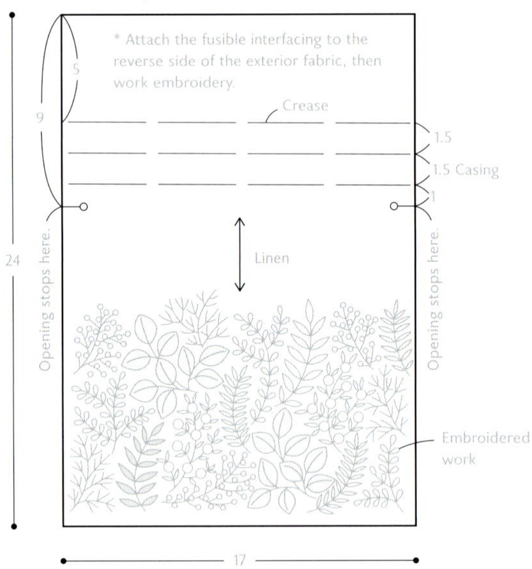

Lining fabric (Cut two pieces.)

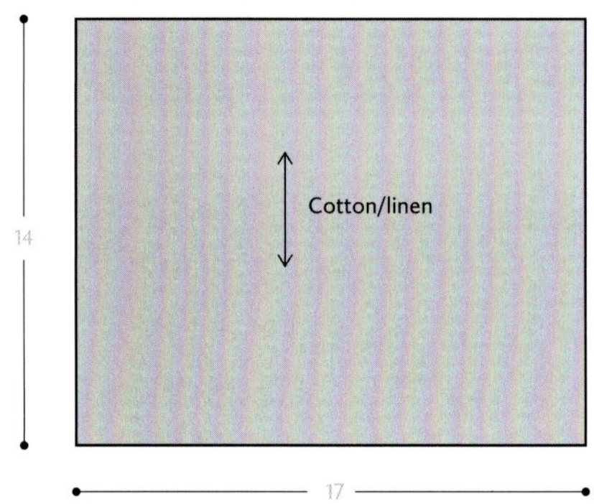

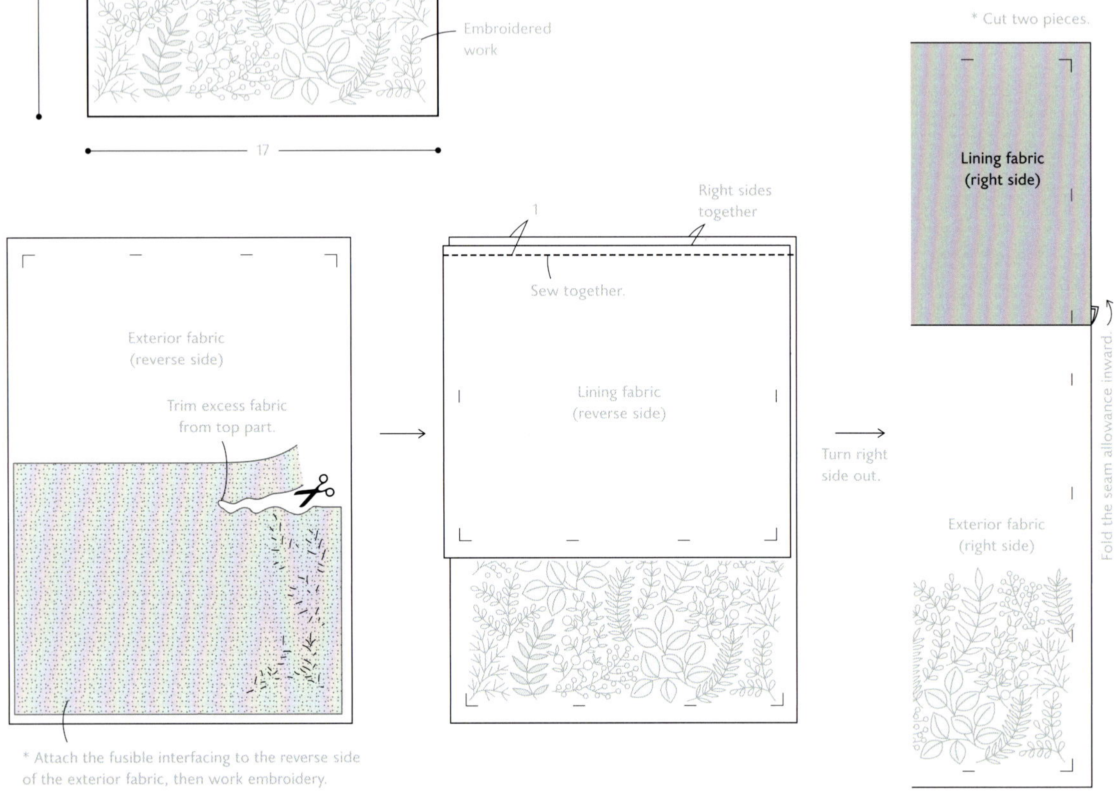

Assemble the two pieces, right sides together.

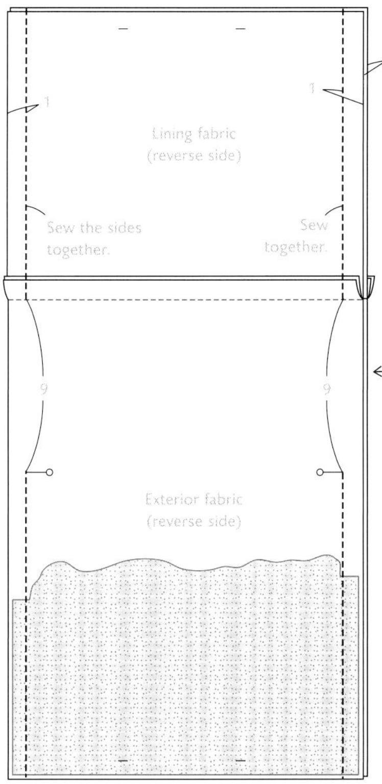

Sew the opening.

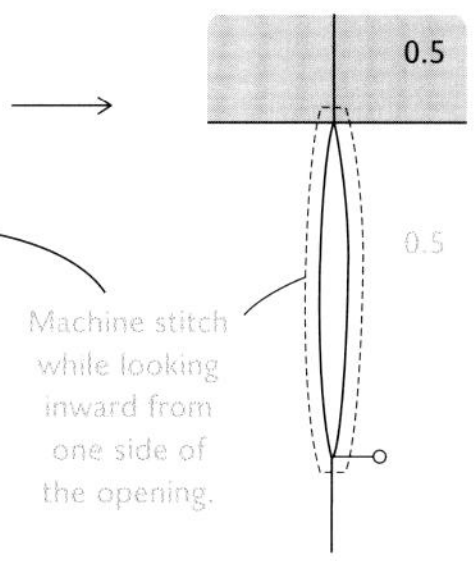

Sew the bottom onto the pouch.

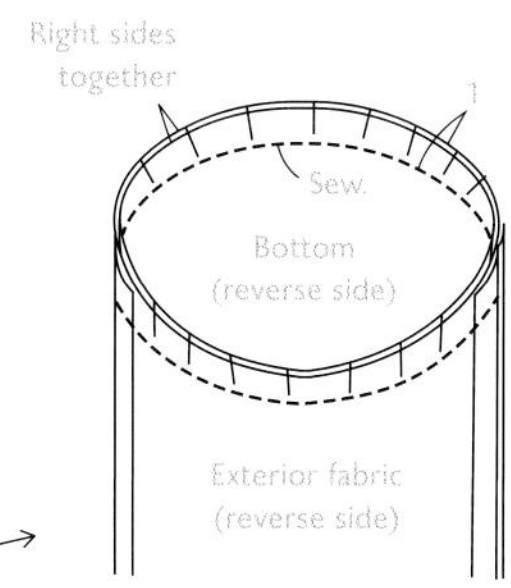

* Repeat for the lining fabric.

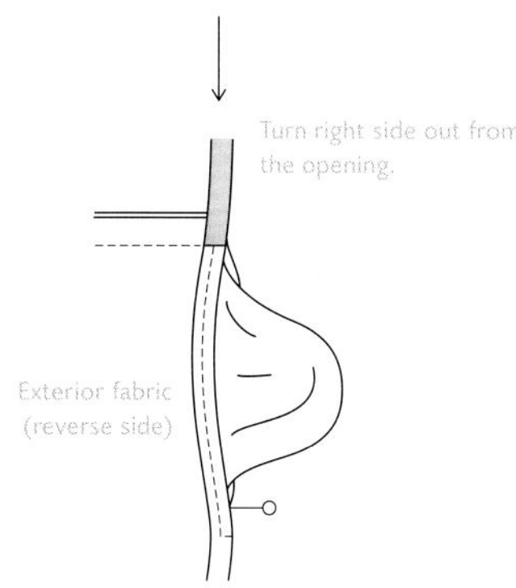

Make the casings.

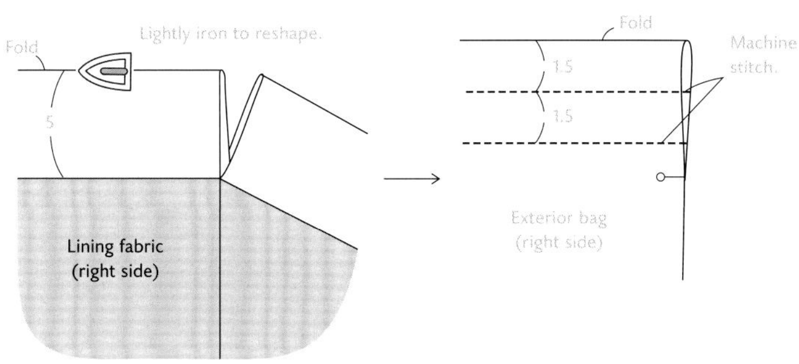

Cut the cord into two 60-cm pieces and pass one through each casing.

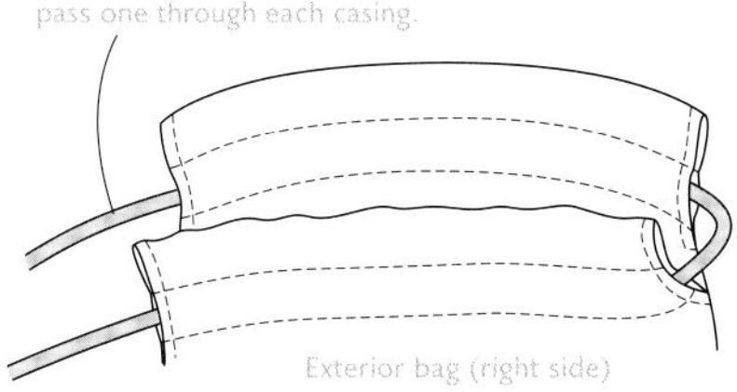

FINISHED PROJECT

4-a 4-b Green Leaves | pp. 8, 9

* Enlarge pattern by 120%.

Project instructions | p. 58 (Round-Bottomed Drawstring Pouch)

11-a 11-b Leaves and Stems | pp. 1, 14

* Enlarge pattern by 120%.

Project instructions | p. 58 (Round-Bottomed Drawstring Pouch)

5 Book Cover | p. 10

Finished measurements: 16 x 30 cm

6 Book Cover | p. 10

Finished measurements: 16 x 30 cm

MATERIALS (TO MAKE ONE COVER)

No. 25 embroidery floss (refer to patterns for color codes)
Fabric: Linen, 30 x 50 cm; printed cotton, 25 x 55 cm
Other: Fusible interfacing, 30 x 60 cm
* Add a 1-cm seam allowance.
* Attach the fusible interfacing to the reverse side of the linen, then work embroidery.

Main body (Cut one each for the exterior fabric and lining fabric.)

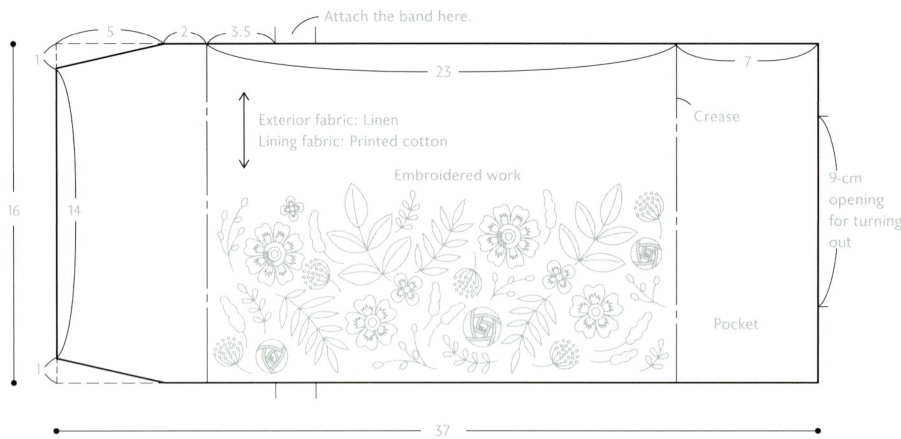

Band (Cut two.)

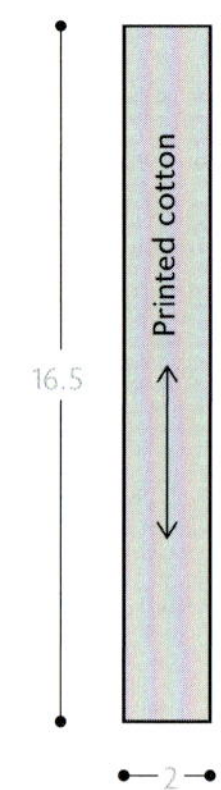

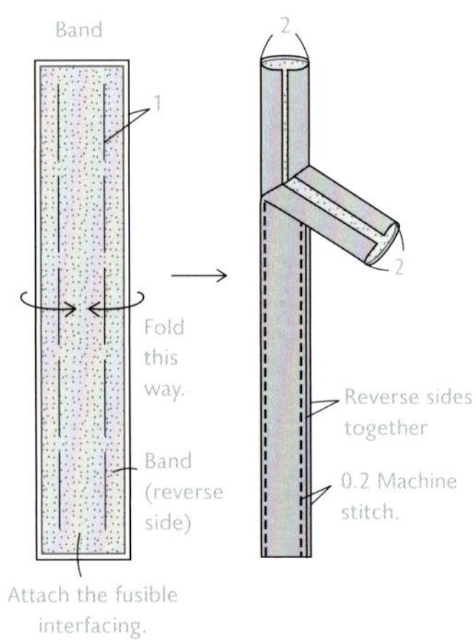

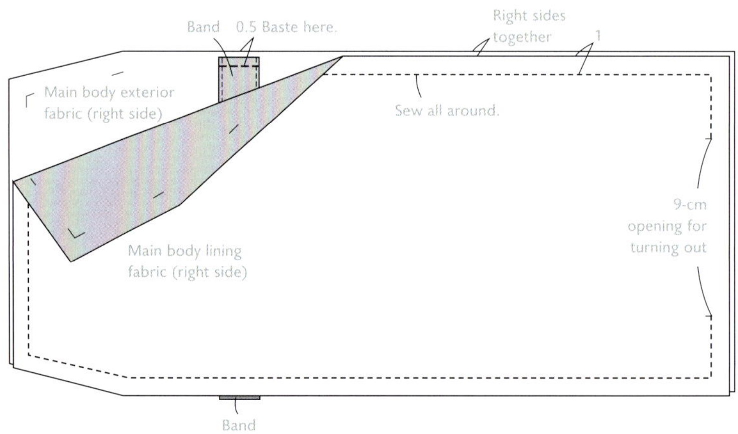

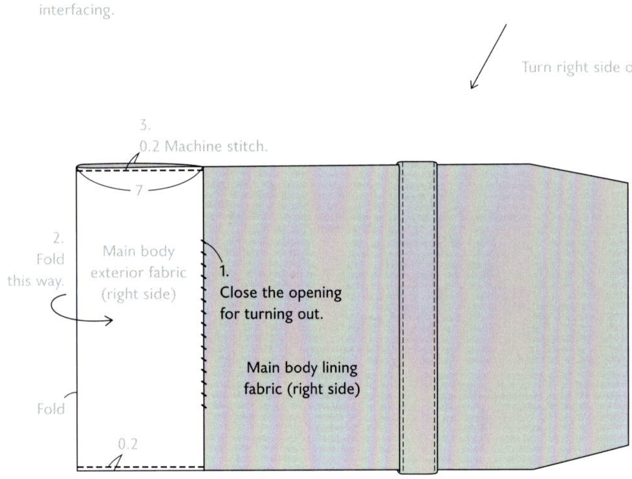

FINISHED PROJECT

Actual size

5

6

10-a Pouches (Flowerpots) | p. 13

Finished measurements: (Large) 15 x 21 cm
(Medium) 11 x 15 cm
(Small) 9 x 11 cm

MATERIALS

No. 25 embroidery floss (refer to patterns for color codes)

(Large) Fabric: Linen, green, 50 x 35 cm; cotton, 45 x 30 cm

Other: Fusible interfacing, 25 x 25 cm; 20-cm-long zipper, 1 piece; stay tape, 45 cm

(Medium) Fabric: Linen, black, 40 x 30 cm; cotton, 35 x 25 cm

Other: Fusible interfacing, 20 x 20 cm; 14-cm-long zipper, 1 piece; stay tape, 35 cm

(Small) Fabric: Linen, brown, 35 x 25 cm; cotton, 30 x 20 cm

Other: Fusible interfacing, 15 x 15 cm; 10-cm-long zipper, 1 piece; stay tape, 25 cm

(Large) Exterior fabric (Cut two pieces.)

(Cut two pieces for the inner lining using the same measurements.)

* Attach the fusible interfacing to the reverse side of the linen, then work embroidery.
* Add a 1-cm seam allowance.

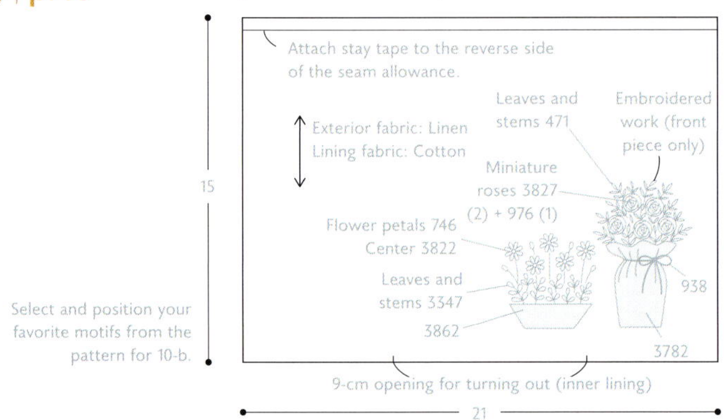

(Medium) Exterior fabric

(Cut two pieces for inner lining using same measurements.)

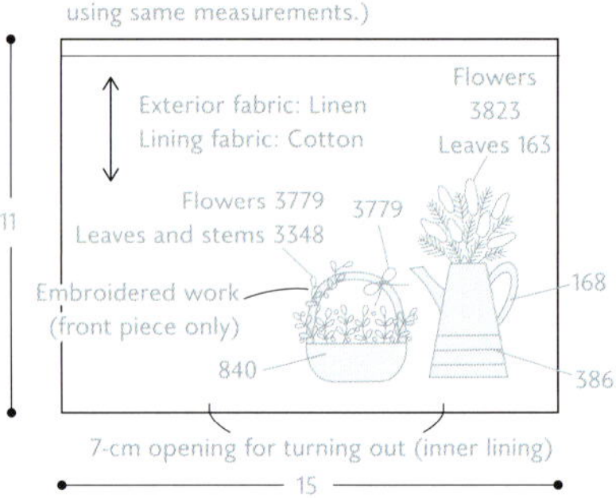

(Small) Exterior fabric

(Cut two pieces for inner lining using same measurements.)

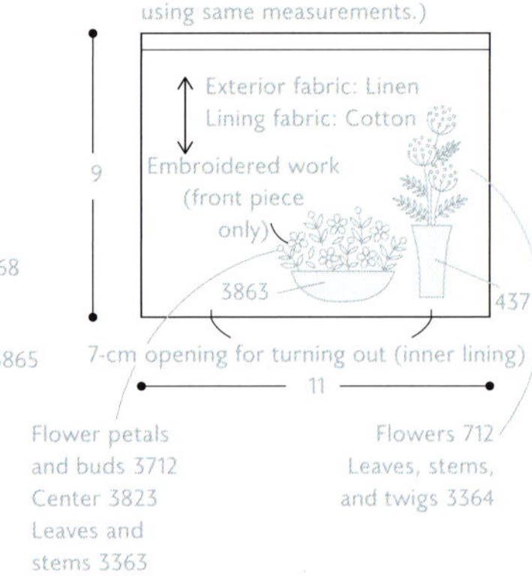

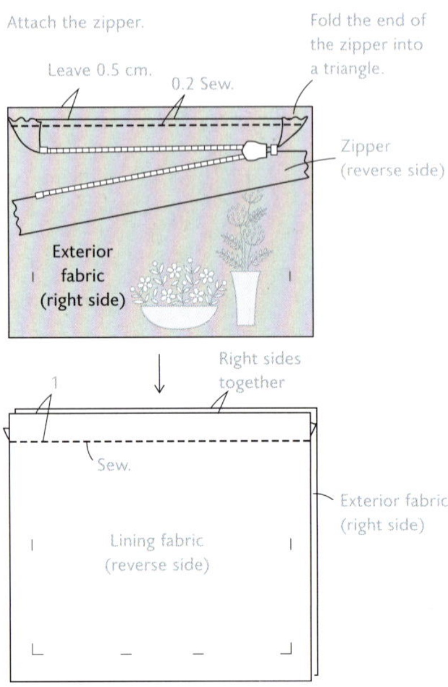

* Repeat on the other side, sewing the zipper the same way.

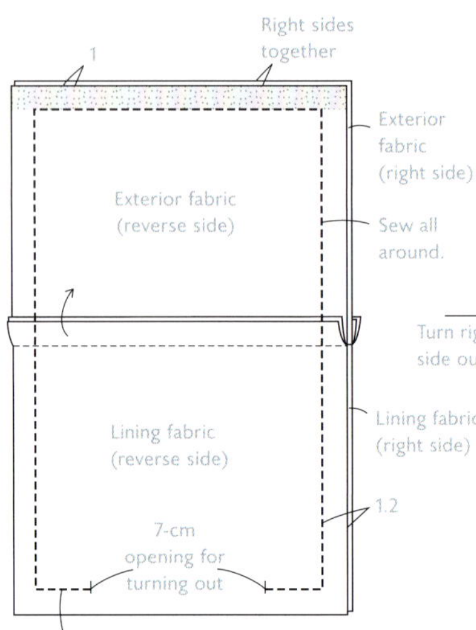

* Sew 0.2 cm inside of the seam allowance.

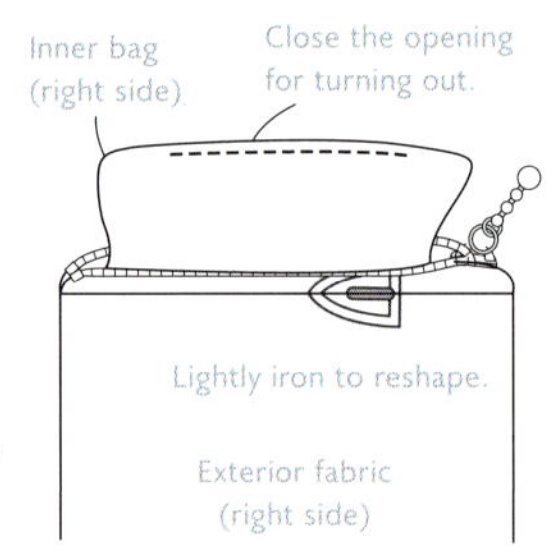

FINISHED PROJECT

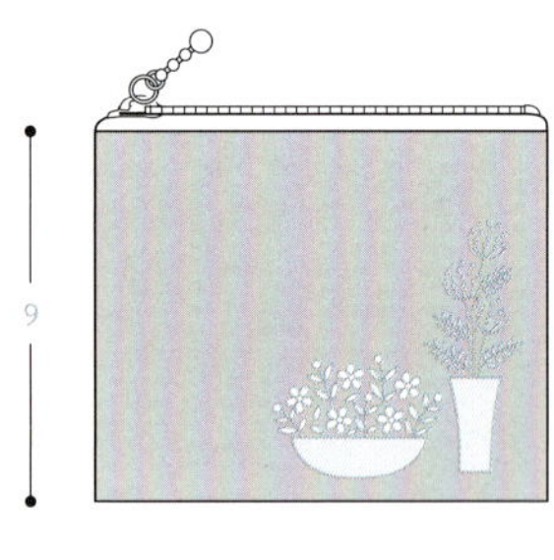

10-b Flowerpots | p. 39

Actual size

* Work chain stitch unless noted otherwise.

▭ For shaded portions, work the border using outline stitch, then fill in using chain stitch (2 strands).

12 Baby's Breath | p. 14

Actual size

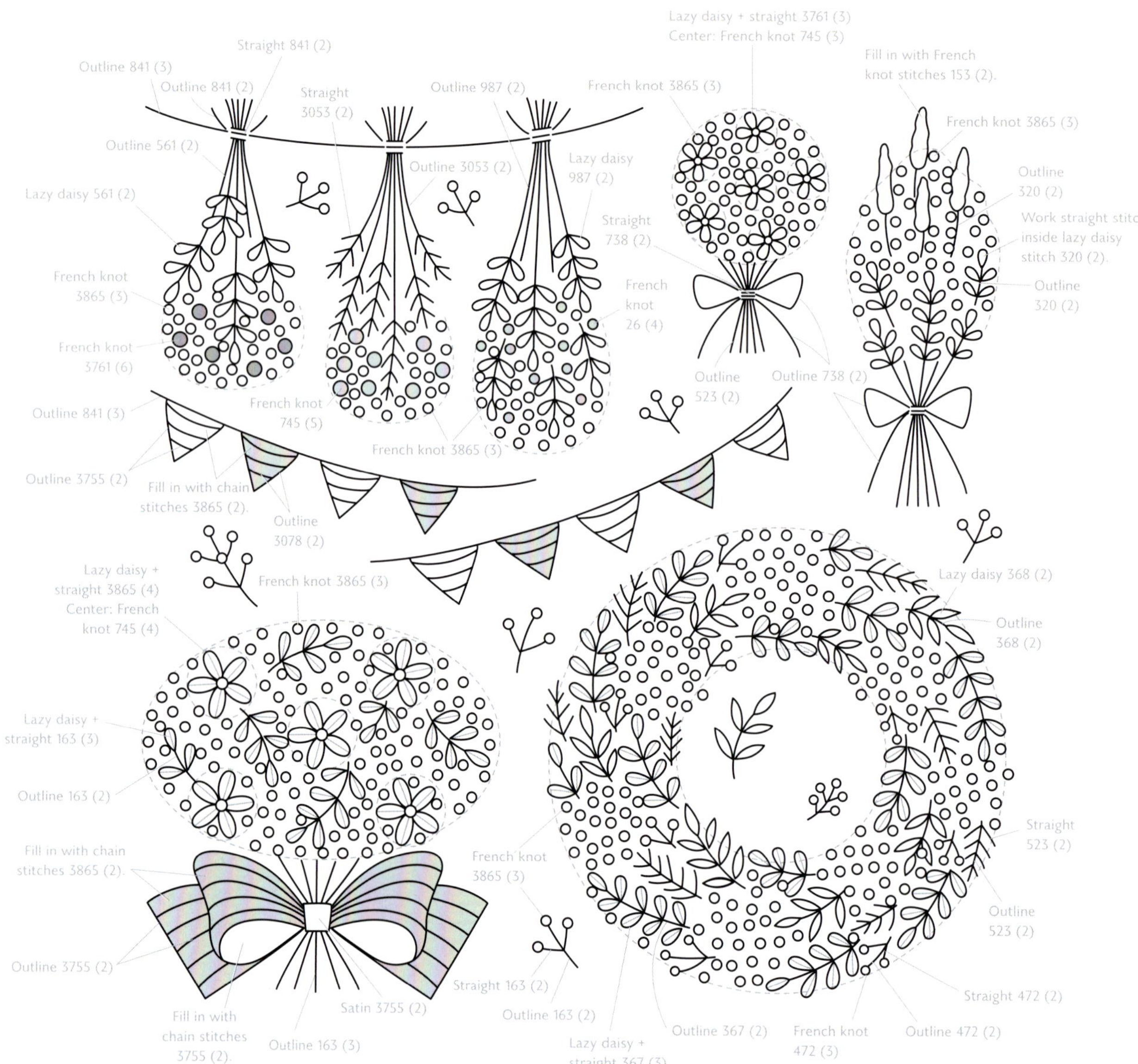

13 A Path Through the Forest | p. 16

* Enlarge pattern by 120%.

* Work chain stitch unless noted otherwise.

14 Kitchen | p. 19

Actual size

* Fill in with chain stitches (2 strands) unless noted otherwise.

15 Breakfast | p. 20

Actual size

16-a Pot Holder (Vegetables) | p. 21

Finished measurements: Height 10 cm x diameter 10 cm

MATERIALS (TO MAKE ONE POT HOLDER)

No. 25 embroidery floss (refer to pattern for color codes)

Fabric: Linen, blue, 25 x 55 cm

Other: Fusible interfacing, 15 x 25 cm; fusible quilt batting, 20 x 25 cm

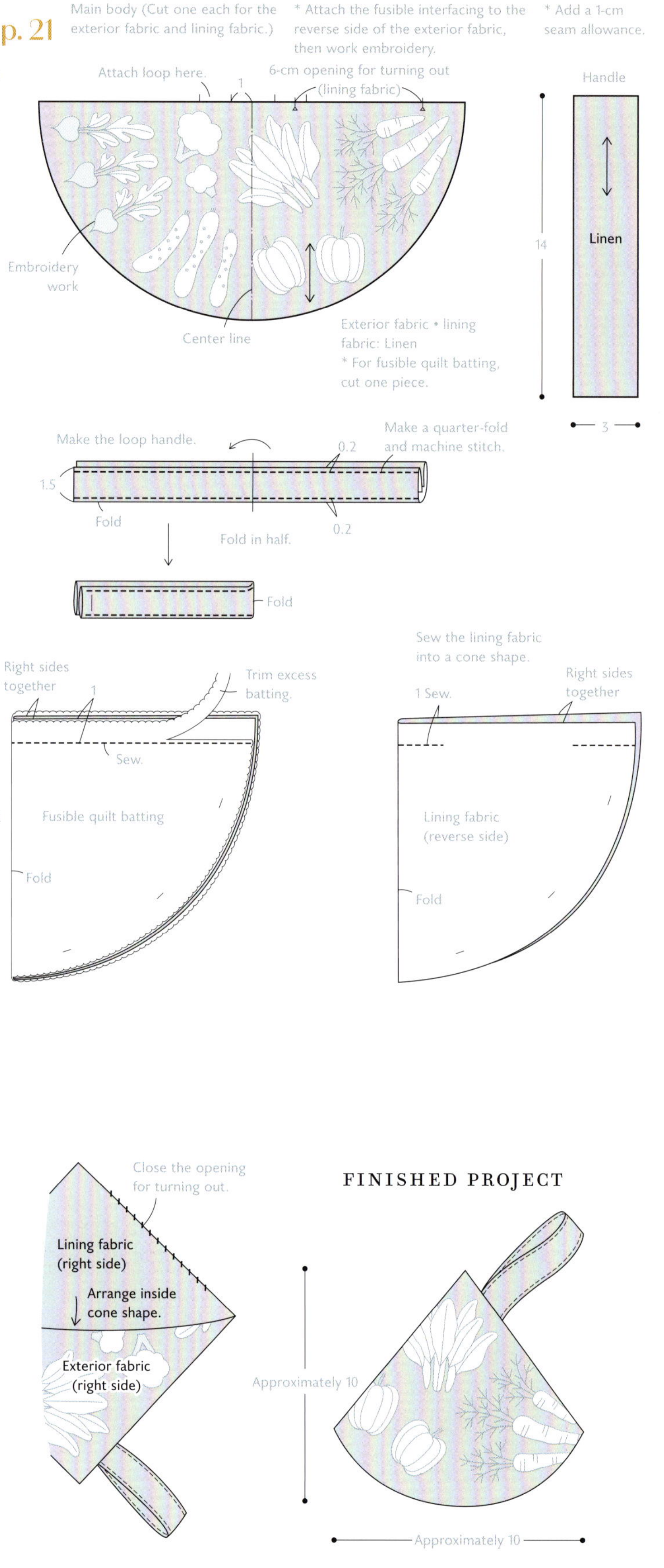

Actual size

For shaded portions, work the border using outline stitch, then fill in using chain stitch 712 (2).

16-b Vegetables | p. 41

p. 41

For shaded portions, work the border using outline stitch, then fill in using chain stitch (2 strands).

Actual size

17-a 17-b Socks | pp. 22, 42

Actual size

17-a
Unless noted otherwise, work the border using outline stitch (3 strands), then fill in using chain stitch (2 strands).

17-b
All stitches are worked using 3866 (white, 3 skeins) and 3687 (pink).
Use 3866 unless noted otherwise. Work the border using outline stitch (3 strands).
For shaded portions, fill in using chain stitch (2 strands).
For stars, use the same number of strands as for 17-a.
For lines, work using 3687 and the same number of strands as for 17-a.

18 Stationery | p. 24

All stitches worked using 712 (3 skeins) unless noted otherwise.
If not specified, work all stitches as outline stitch.
For shaded portions, fill in with chain stitch (2 strands).

Actual size

22 Cherries | p. 29

Requires 2 skeins each of embroidery floss 304 and 367.

* Enlarge pattern by 150%.

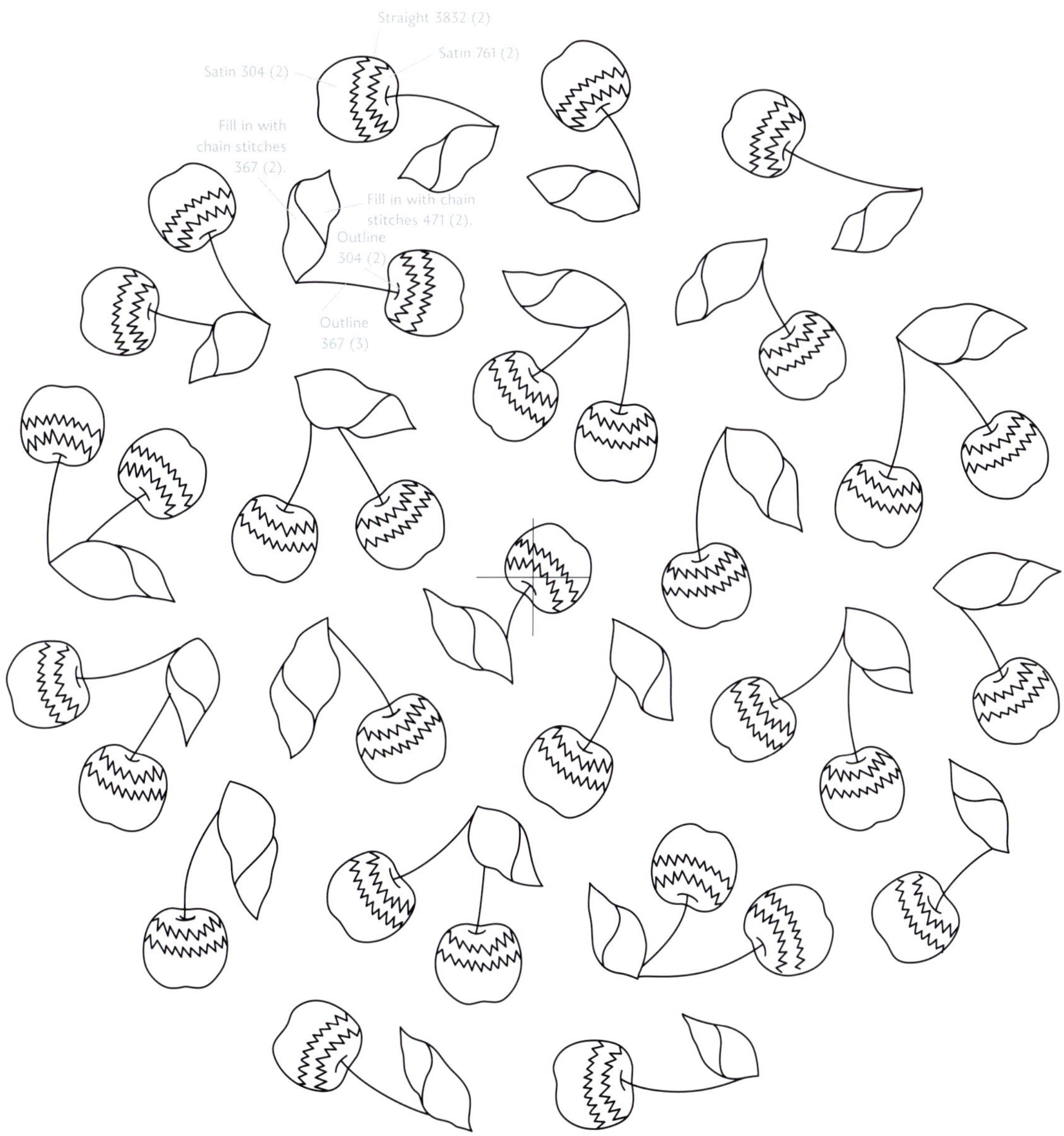

19-a Welcome | p. 25

For shaded portions, work the border using outline stitch,
then fill in using chain stitch (2 strands).
For all doorknobs, work French knot stitch (3 strands).
Work all stitches using ECRU unless noted otherwise.

Actual size

19-b Welcome | p. 43

For shaded portions, work the border using outline stitch, then fill in using chain stitch (2 strands).
For all doorknobs, work French knot stitch 938 (3).

Actual size

20-a Knitted Hats | p. 26

All stitches worked using 3866 (2 skeins) unless noted otherwise.

Actual size

20-b Knitted Hats | p. 43

Work the border using outline stitch, then fill in using chain stitch (2 strands), unless noted otherwise.

Actual size

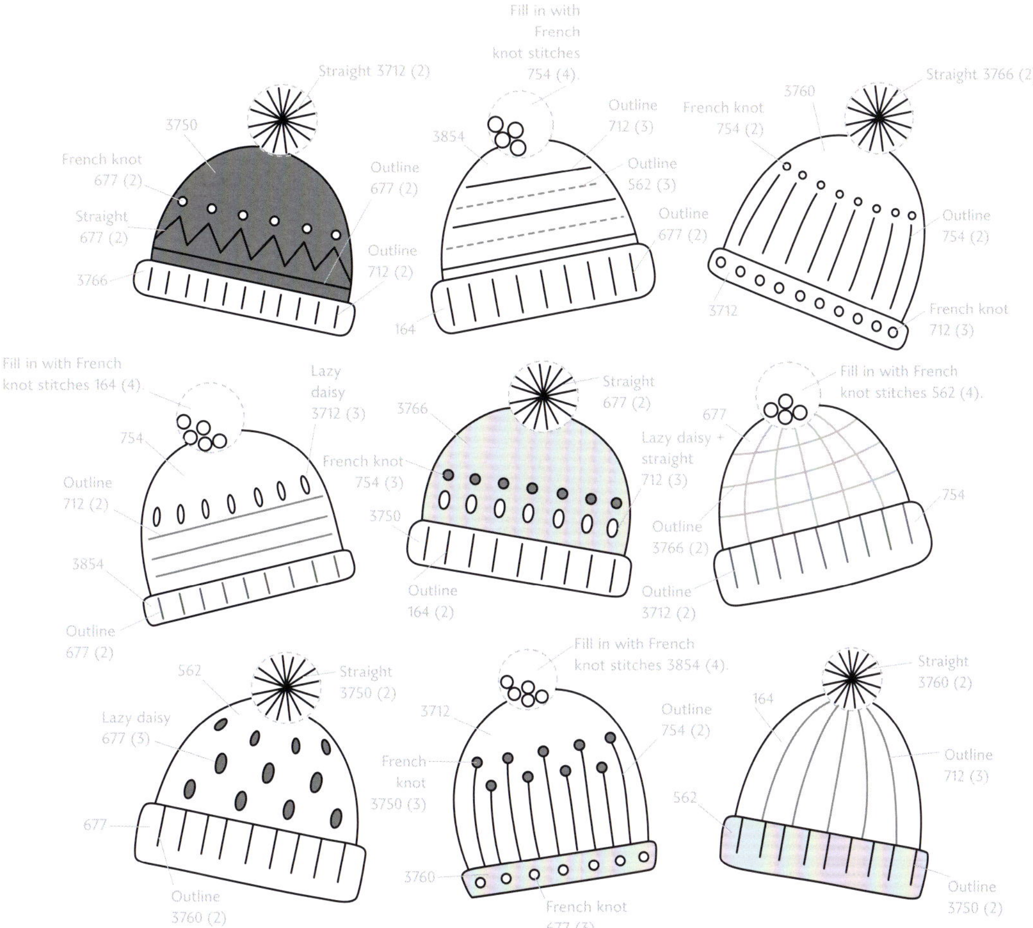

21-b Cup Holder | p. 27

Pattern | pp. 80, 81

Finished measurements: Height approximately 7 cm

MATERIALS (TO MAKE ONE HOLDER)

No. 25 embroidery floss
(refer to pattern for color codes)

Fabric: Linen, dark grey, 35 x 35 cm

Other: Fusible interfacing, 20 x 35 cm;
2.5-cm-wide Velcro tape, 4 cm

MAIN BODY

(Cut one each for exterior fabric and lining fabric.) (One color)

* Add 1-cm seam allowance.

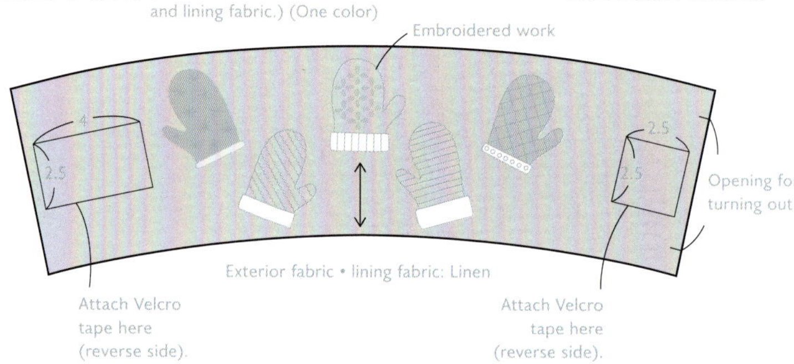

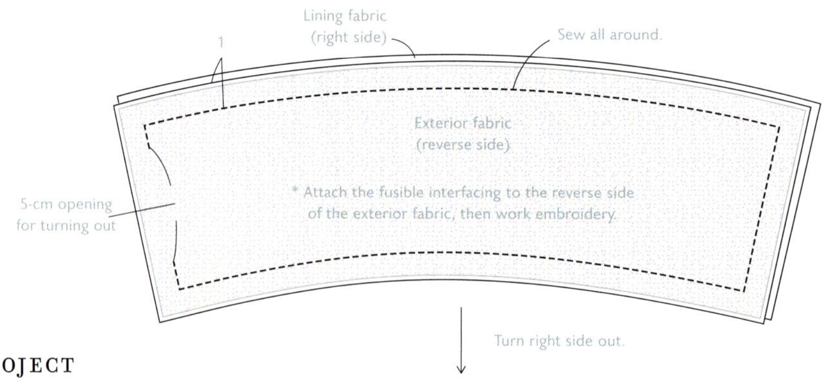

FINISHED PROJECT

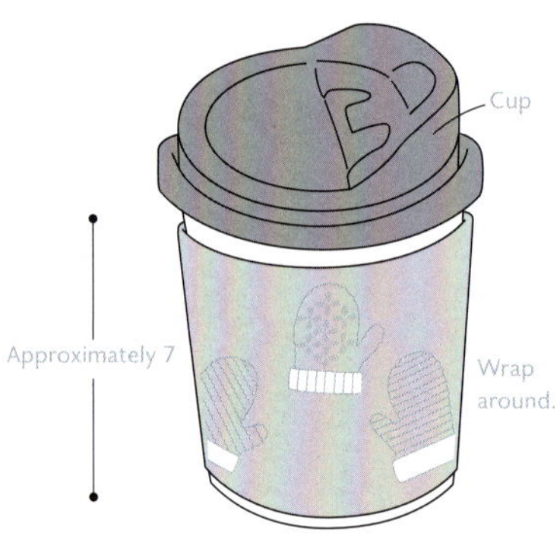

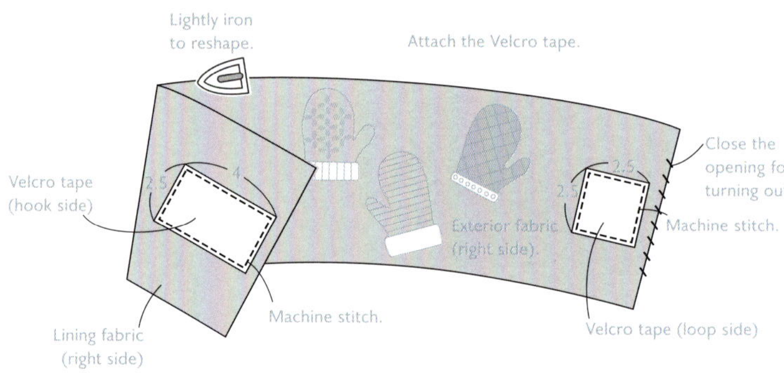

For shaded portions, fill in with chain stitch (2 strands). Work all stitches using 712 (white) unless noted otherwise.

One color
Enlarge pattern by 180%.

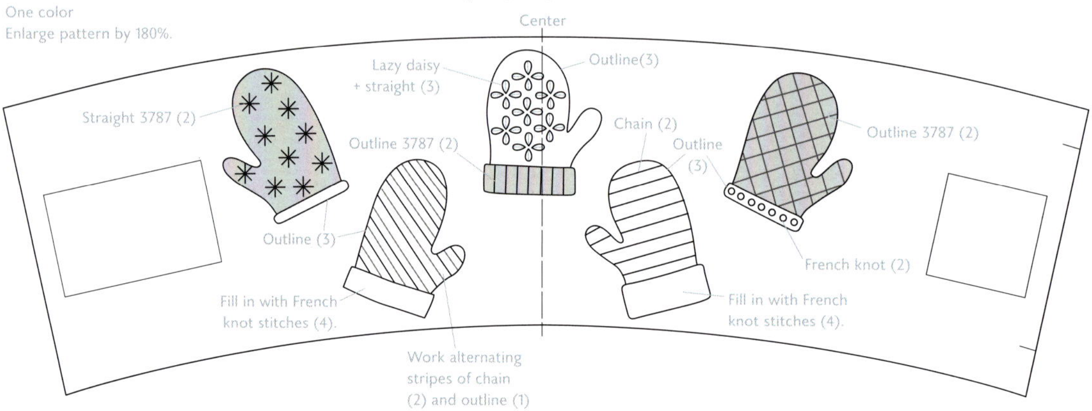

21-a Mittens | p. 27

Work all stitches using 3865 (white, 2 skeins) unless noted otherwise.

Actual size

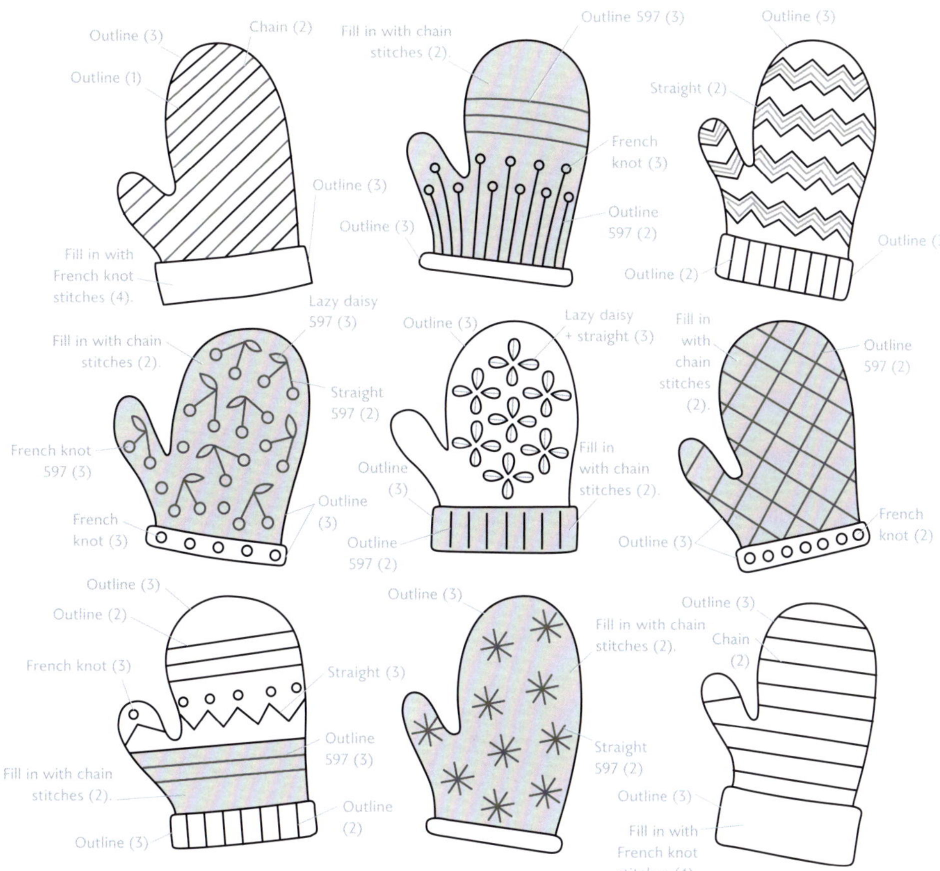

21-b Cup Holder (multicolor)

Fill in with chain stitch (2 strands) unless noted otherwise.

Enlarge pattern by 180%.

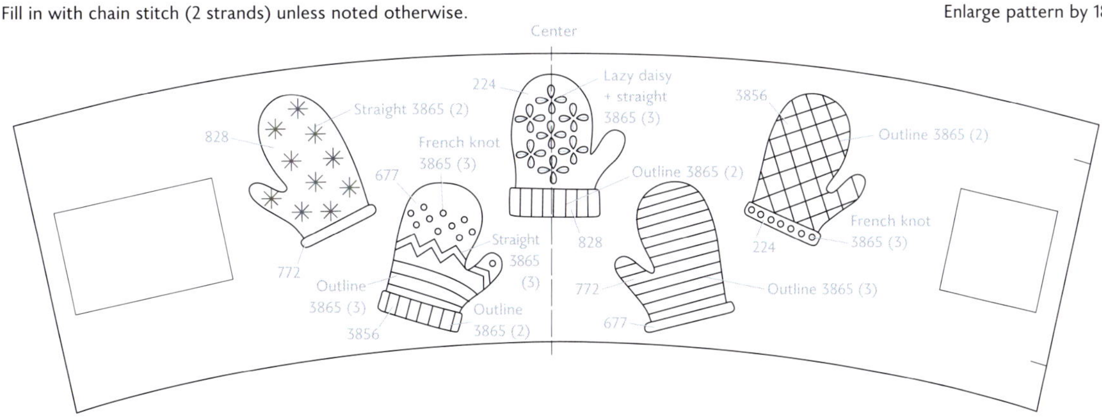

21-C Mittens | p. 42

Actual size

23 Bread | p. 30

Fill in with chain stitch (2 strands) unless noted otherwise.

Actual size

24-a Magnets (Sweet Treats) | p. 30

For shaded portions, work the border using outline stitch, then fill in using chain stitch (2 strands).

Actual size

HOW TO MAKE THE MAGNET

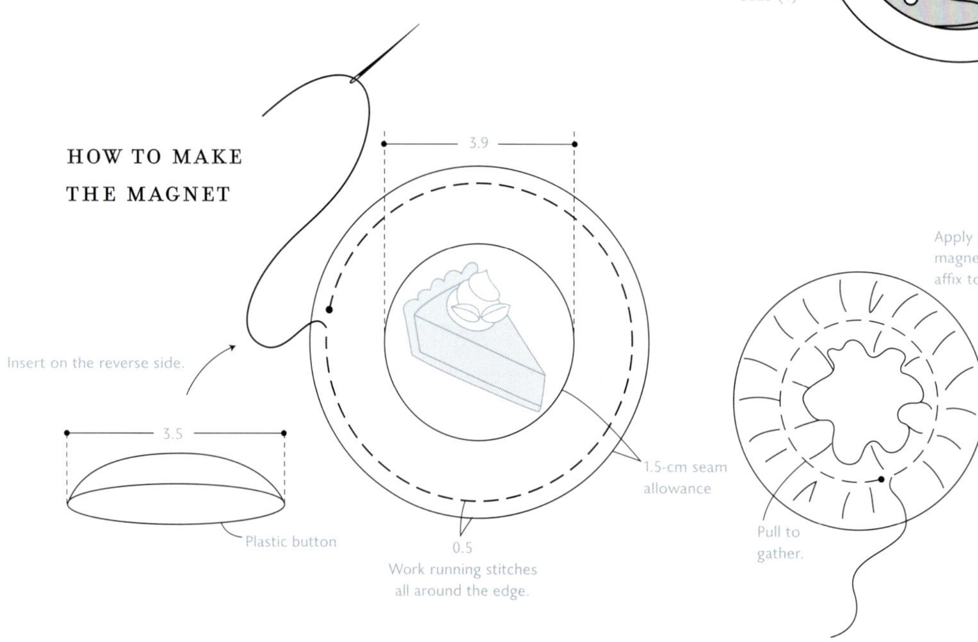

24-b Sweet Treats | p. 41

For shaded portions, work the border using outline stitch, then fill in using chain stitch (2 strands).

Actual size

25-a Ribbon (Mushrooms) | p. 32

For shaded portions, work the border using outline stitch, then fill in using chain stitch (2 strands).

Actual size
Use a 7.7-cm-wide grosgrain ribbon.

25-b Drawstring Pouch (Mushrooms) | p. 33

Project instructions | pp. 88, 89

Actual size

9 Drawstring Pouch (Florets) | p. 12

Pattern | p. 56
Finished measurements: 14 x 10 cm

MATERIALS

No. 25 embroidery floss (refer to pattern for color codes)

Fabric: Exterior fabric, linen, pink, 35 x 35 cm; lining fabric, cotton, 20 x 35 cm

Other: Fusible interfacing, 15 x 15 cm; cord, 80 cm

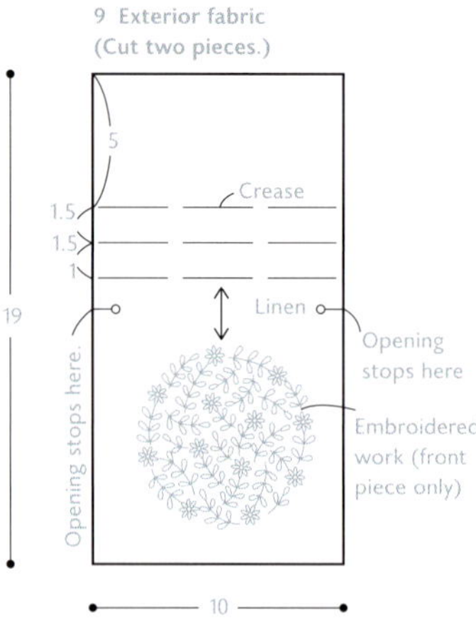

* Add a 1-cm seam allowance.
* Attach the fusible interfacing to the reverse side of the linen, then work embroidery.

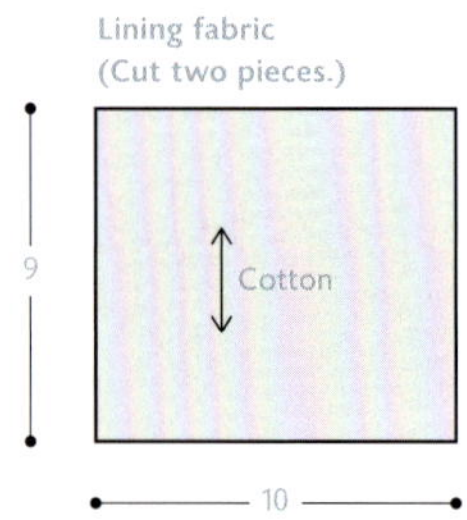

25-b Drawstring Pouch (Mushrooms)

Pattern | p. 87
Finished measurements: 18.5 x 12 cm x (gusset) 5 cm

MATERIALS

No. 25 embroidery floss (refer to pattern for color codes)

Fabric: Exterior fabric, linen, brown, 40 x 50 cm; lining fabric, cotton, 25 x 45 cm

Other: Fusible interfacing, 20 x 20 cm; cord, 100 cm

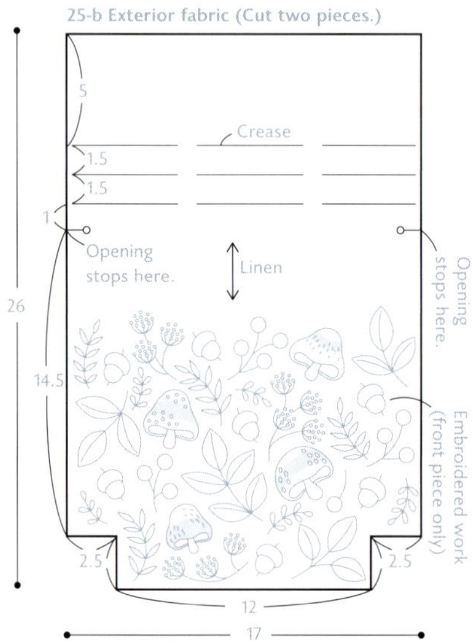

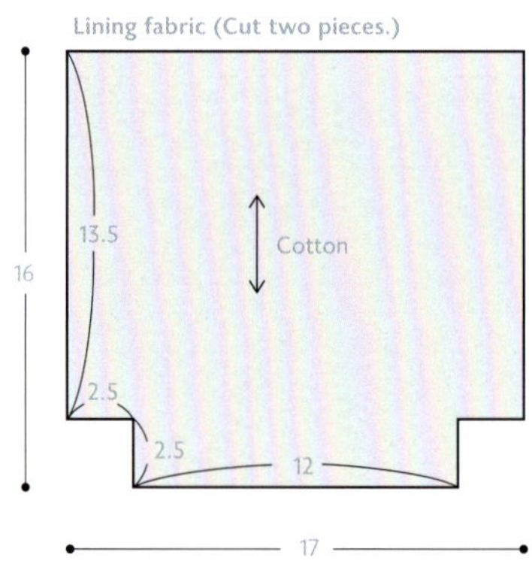

26 Drawstring Pouch (Watermelon) | p. 34

Pattern | p. 90
Finished measurements:
15 x 13 cm x (gusset) 7 cm

MATERIALS

No. 25 embroidery floss (refer to pattern for color codes)

Fabric: Exterior fabric, linen, blue, 35 x 60 cm; lining fabric, cotton, 35 x 25 cm

Other: Fusible interfacing, 25 x 25 cm; cord, 120 cm

27 Drawstring Pouch (Pears) | p. 34

Pattern | p. 90
Finished measurements: 18 x 15 cm x (gusset) 10 cm

MATERIALS

No. 25 embroidery floss (refer to pattern for color codes)

Fabric: Exterior fabric, linen, white, 40 x 70 cm; lining fabric, cotton, 45 x 30 cm

Other: Fusible interfacing, 30 x 30 cm; cord, 140 cm

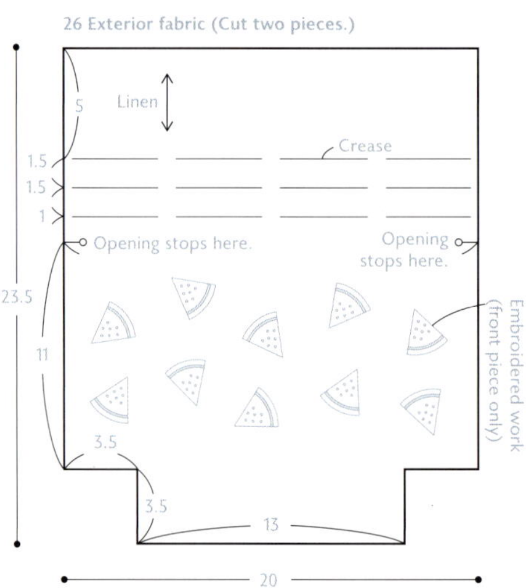

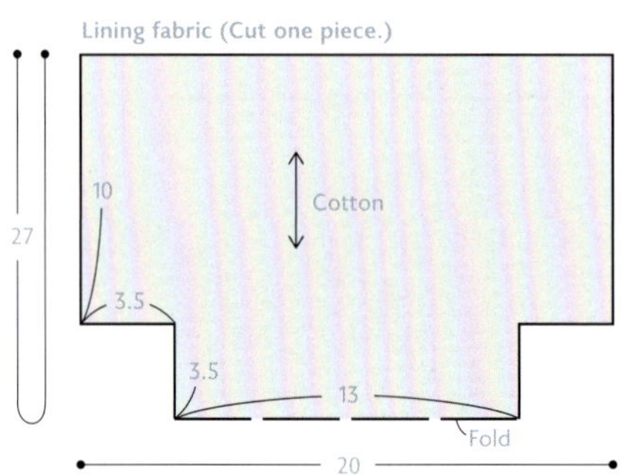

27 Exterior fabric (Cut two pieces.)

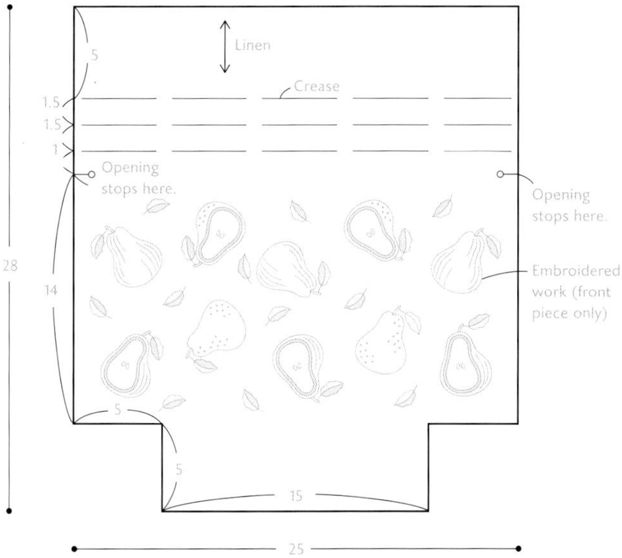

27 Lining fabric (Cut one piece.)

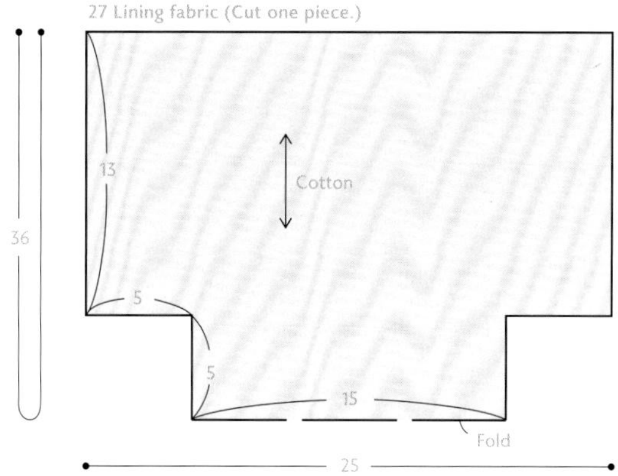

How to Make 25-b

* Follow same instructions for 9, 26, 27.

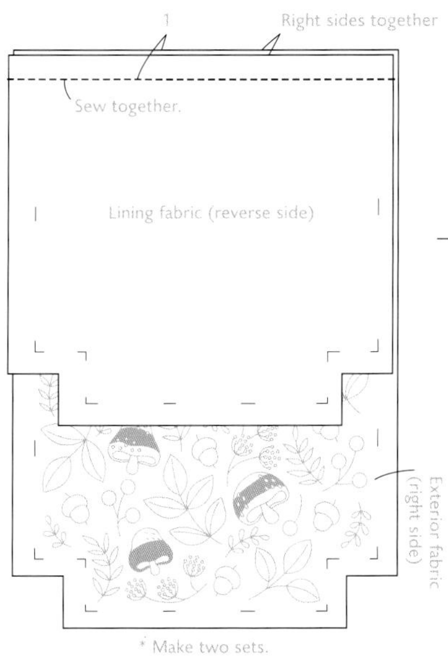

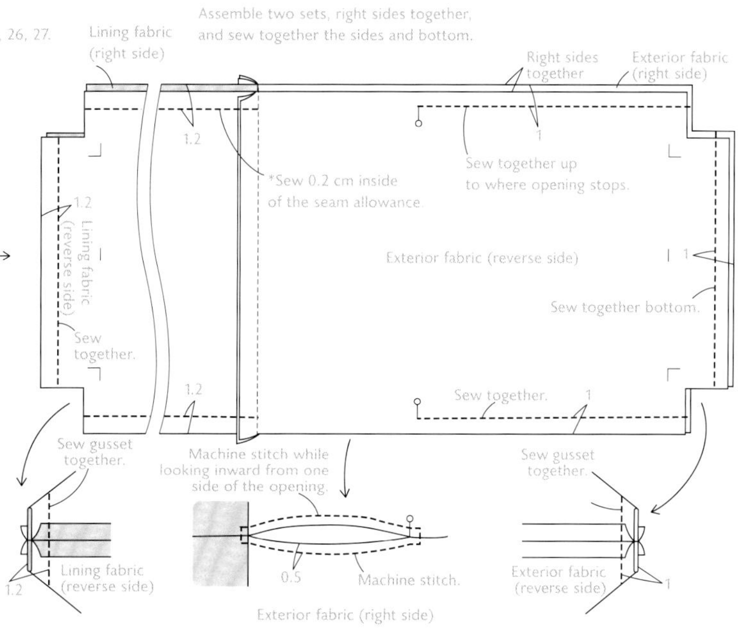

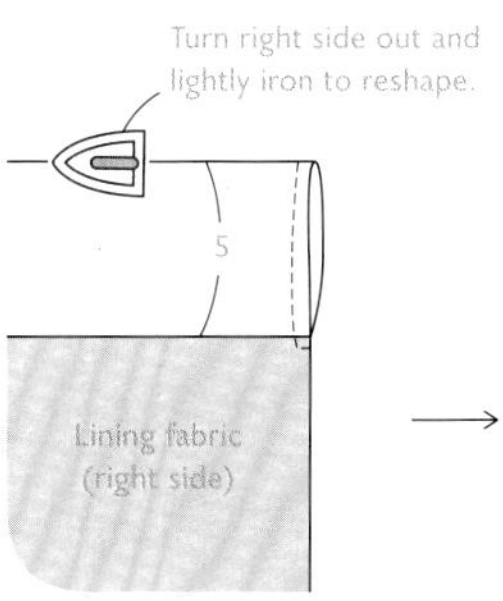

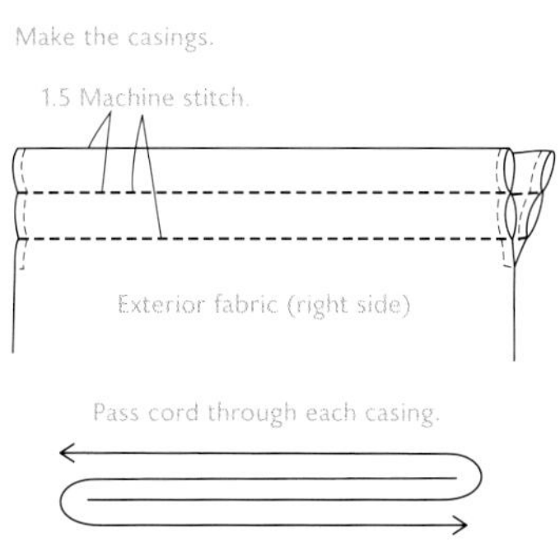

Finished Project

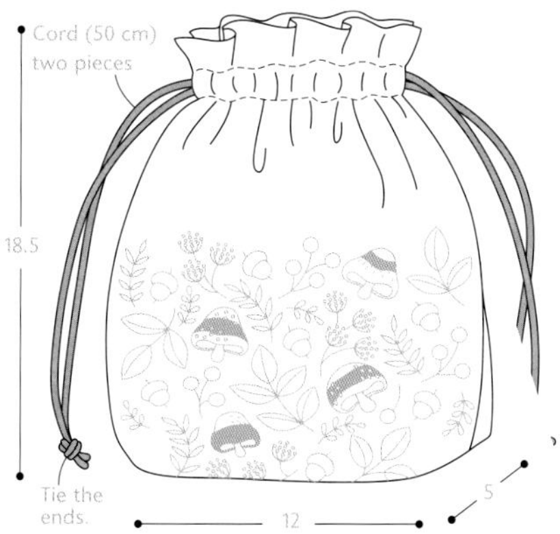

25-b Drawstring Pouch (Watermelon) (Pears) | p. 34

Project instructions | pp. 88, 89

Enlarge pattern by 160%.

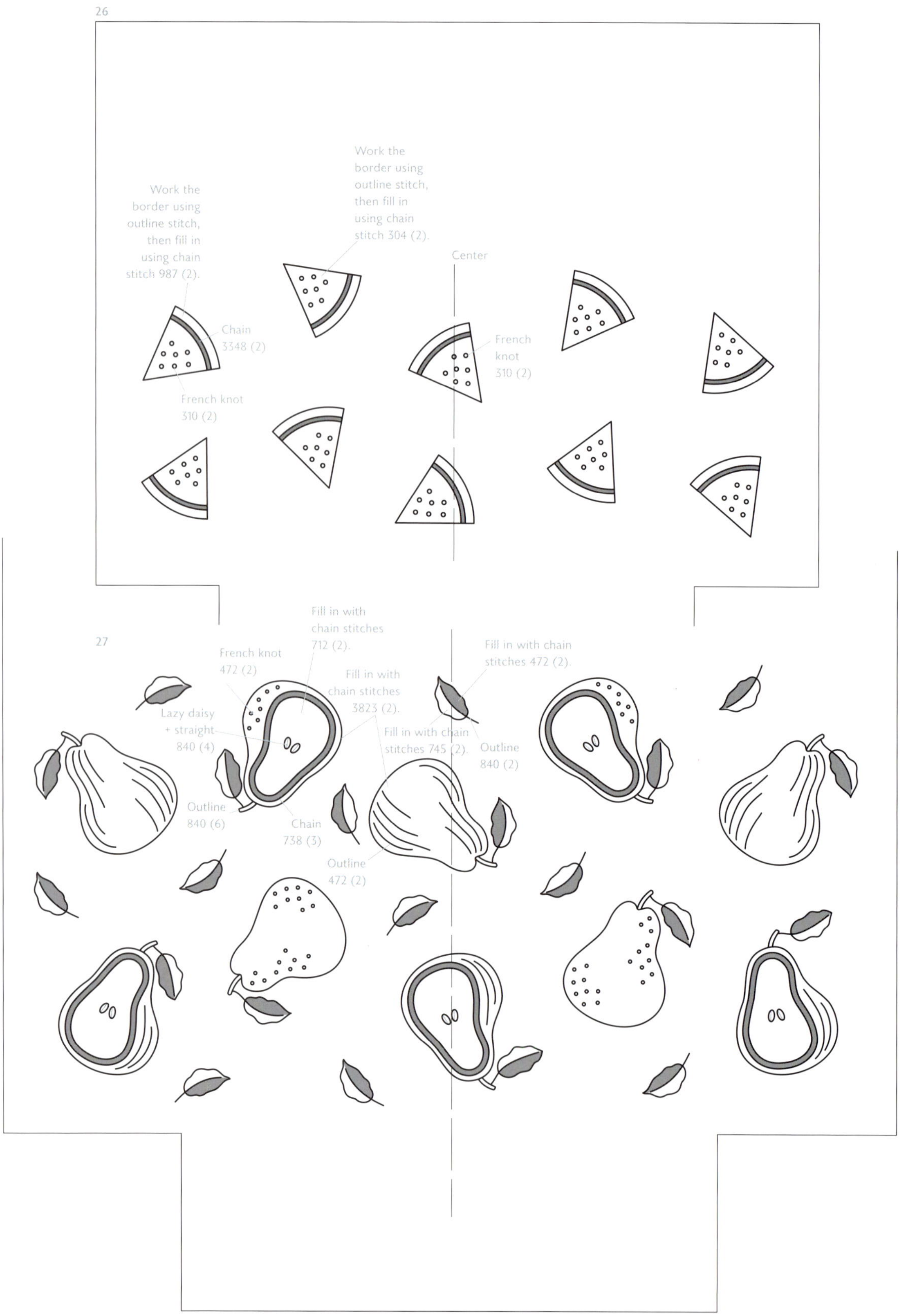

28 Atelier | p. 37

For shaded portions, work the border using outline stitch, then fill in using chain stitch (2 strands). For all other stitches, work outline stitch unless noted otherwise.

Actual size

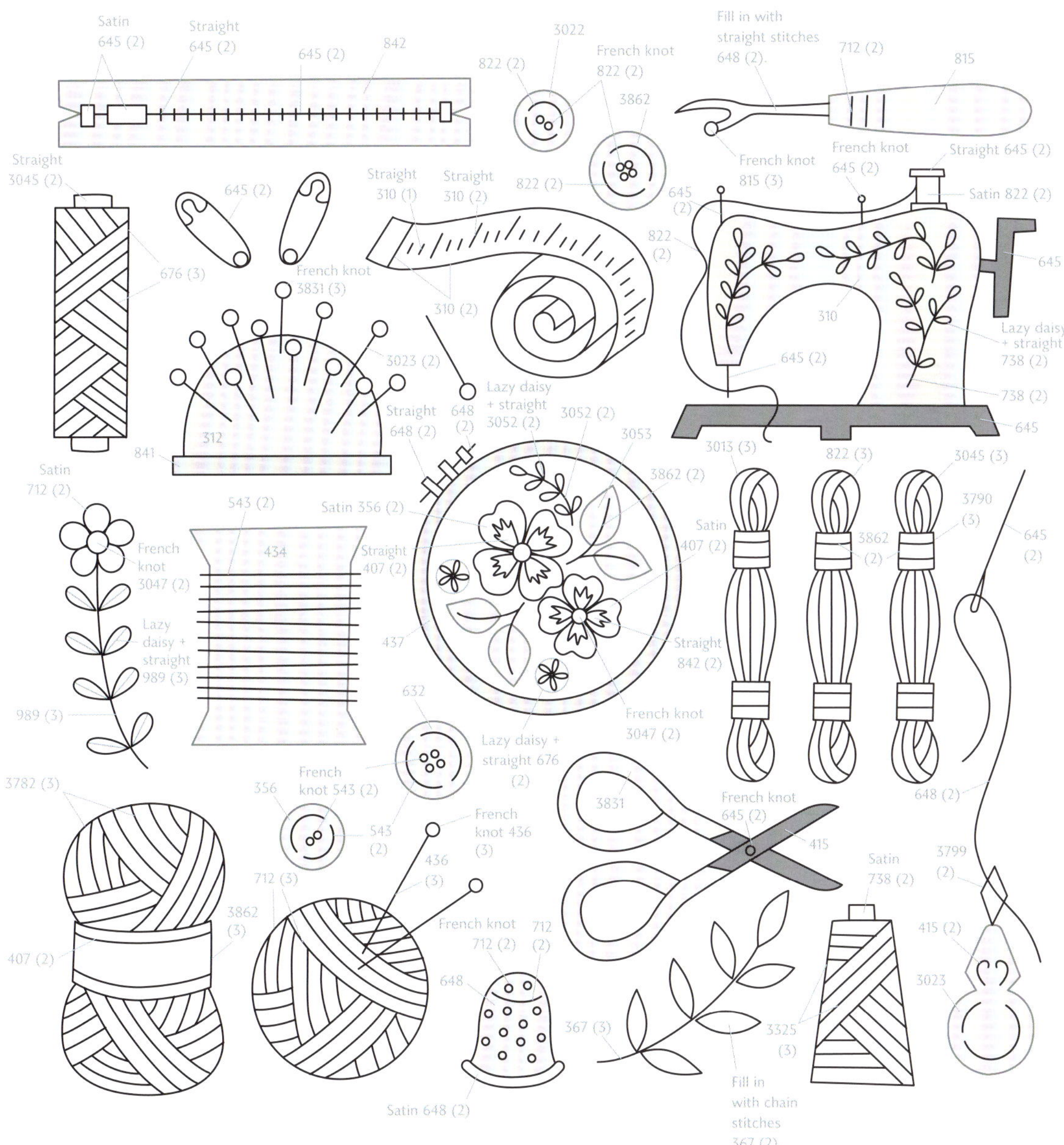

29 Gardening | p. 37

Fill in with chain stitches (2 strands) unless noted otherwise.

Actual size

30 Cookies | p. 38

Fill in with chain stitches unless noted otherwise.

Actual size

31 Bakery | p. 38

Fill in with chain stitches (2 strands) unless noted otherwise.

Actual size

32 Teatime | p. 39

For shaded portions, work the border using outline stitch, then fill in using chain stitch (2 strands). For all other stitches, work outline stitch unless noted otherwise.

Actual size

YULA

Yula is an embroidery artist. After graduating from fashion school, she worked as a designer for an apparel company. Following her marriage, she started making handmade items as a hobby, and in 2016 she launched her Instagram with an emphasis on embroidery. Now, with over 160,000 followers, she continues to post regularly about her embroidery projects. Yula adores creating embroidery and needle arts projects with an attention to detail and vivid colors. Her Instagram is @yula-handmade_2008.

Roost Books
An imprint of Shambhala Publications, Inc.
2129 13th Street
Boulder, Colorado 80302
www.shambhala.com

Translation by Allison Markin Powell
Originally published as *Yura no shiawase no shishuu: watashi no suki na mono* © 2023 by Yula / NIHON VOGUE-SHA

NIHON VOGUE STAFF CREDITS

Photography: Tadaaki Omori
English translation rights arranged with NIHON VOGUE Corp. through Japan UNI Agency Inc., Tokyo.

9 8 7 6 5 4 3 2 1

First English edition
Printed in China

Shambhala Publications makes every effort to print on acid-free, recycled paper.
Shambhala Publications is distributed worldwide by Penguin Random House, Inc., and its subsidiaries.

Library of Congress Cataloging-in-Publication Data
Names: Yula (Embroidery artist) author
Title: Embroidering happiness: patterns and projects for life's everyday treasures / Yula; translation by Allison Markin Powell.
Other titles: Yura no shiawase no shishuu. English S
Description: Boulder, Colorado: Roost Books, [2026] | Translation of: Yura no shiawase no shishuu: watashi no suki na mono. | Text in English. Translated from Japanese.
Identifiers: LCCN 2025037998 | ISBN 9781645474371 trade paperback
Subjects: LCSH: Embroidery—Patterns
Classification: LCC TT771 .Y84913 2026 | DDC 746.44041—dc23/eng/20251125
LC record available at https://lccn.loc.gov/2025037998

The authorized representative in the EU for product safety and compliance is eucomply OÜ, Pärnu mnt 139b-14, 11317 Tallinn, Estonia, hello@eucompliancepartner.com.